Here, Now
And Beyond

Oxford English Source Books

BOOK 1
Here, Now And Beyond

BOOK 2
Truth To Tell

BOOK 3
Half-way

Here, Now And Beyond

Nancy Martin

OXFORD UNIVERSITY PRESS

Oxford University Press, Ely House, London W1
GLASGOW NEW YORK TORONTO MELBOURNE WELLINGTON
CAPE TOWN IBADAN NAIROBI DAR ES SALAAM LUSAKA ADDIS ABABA
DELHI BOMBAY CALCUTTA MADRAS KARACHI LAHORE DACCA
KUALA LUMPUR SINGAPORE HONG KONG TOKYO

FIRST PUBLISHED 1968
REPRINTED (WITH CORRECTIONS) 1970, 1972

PRINTED IN GREAT BRITAIN
AT THE UNIVERSITY PRESS, OXFORD
BY VIVIAN RIDLER
PRINTER TO THE UNIVERSITY

CONTENTS

MY WORLD

OTHER WORLDS

NO BOUNDARIES

MY WORLD

1. My Friends and Me

Here is a story to start you talking. It is by an American writer named William Saroyan.

The Great Leapfrog Contest

Rosie Mahoney was a tough little Irish kid whose folks had moved into the Russian-Italian-and-Greek neighbourhood of my home town, across the Southern Pacific tracks, around G Street.

She wore a turtle-neck sweater, usually red. Her father was a bricklayer named Cull and a heavy drinker. Her mother's name was Mary. Mary Mahoney used to go to the Greek Orthodox Catholic Church on Kearny Boulevard every Sunday, because there was no Irish Church to go to anywhere in the neighbourhood. The family seemed to be a happy one.

Rosie's three brothers had all grown up and gone to sea. Her two sisters had married. Rosie was the last of the clan. She had entered the world when her father had been close to sixty and her mother in her early fifties. For all that, she was hardly the studious or scholarly type.

Rosie had little use for girls, and as far as possible avoided them. She had less use for boys, but found it undesirable to avoid them. That is to say, she made it a point to take part in everything the boys did. She was always on hand, and always the first to take up any daring or crazy idea. Everybody felt awkward about her continuous presence, but it was no use trying to chase her away, because that meant a fight in which she asked no quarter, and gave none.

If she didn't whip every boy she fought, every fight was at least an honest draw, with a slight edge in Rosie's favour. She didn't fight girl-style, or cry if hurt. She fought the regular style and took advantage of every opening. It was very humiliating to be hurt by Rosie, so after a while any boy who thought of trying to chase her away, decided not to.

It was no use. She just wouldn't go. She didn't seem to like any of the boys especially, but she liked being in on any mischief they might have in mind, and she wanted to play on any teams they organized. She was an excellent baseball player, being as good as anybody else in the neighbourhood at any position, and for her age an expert pitcher. She had a wicked wing, too, and could throw a ball in from left field so that when it hit the catcher's mitt it made a nice sound.

She was extraordinarily swift on her feet and played a beautiful game of tin-can hockey.

At pee-wee, she seemed to have the most disgusting luck in the world.

At the game we invented and used to call *Horse* she was as good at *horse* as at *rider*, and she insisted on following the rules of the game. She insisted on being horse when it was her turn to be horse. This always embarrassed her partner, whoever he happened to be, because it didn't seem right for a boy to be getting up on the back of a girl.

She was an excellent football player too.

As a matter of fact, she was just naturally the equal of any boy in the neighbourhood, and much the superior of many of them. Especially after she had lived in the neighbourhood three years. It took her that long to make everybody understand that she had come to stay and that she was *going* to stay.

She did, too; even after the arrival of a boy named Rex Folger, who was from somewhere in the south of Texas. This boy Rex was a natural-born leader. Two months after his arrival in the neighbourhood, it was understood by everyone that if Rex wasn't the leader of the gang, he was very nearly the leader. He had fought and licked every boy in the neighbourhood who at one time or another had fancied himself leader. And he had done so without any noticeable ill-feeling, pride or ambition.

As a matter of fact, no-one could possibly have been more good-natured than Rex. Everybody resented him, just the same.

One winter, the whole neighbourhood took to playing a game that had become popular on the other side of the tracks, in another slum neighbourhood of the town: *Leapfrog*. The idea was for as many boys as cared to participate, to bend down and be leaped over by every other boy in the game, and then himself to get up and begin leaping over all the other boys, and then bend down again until all the boys had leaped over him again, and keep this up until all the other players had become exhausted. This didn't happen, sometimes, until the last two players had travelled a distance of three or four miles while the other players walked along, watching and making bets.

Rosie, of course, was always in on the game. She was always one of the last to drop out, too. And she was the only person in the neighbourhood Rex Folger hadn't fought and beaten.

He felt that that was much too humiliating even to think about. But inasmuch as she seemed to be a member of the gang, he felt that in some way or another he ought to prove his superiority.

One summer day during vacation, an argument between Rex and Rosie developed and Rosie pulled off her turtle-neck sweater and challenged him to a fight. Rex told Rosie he wasn't in the habit of hitting women—where he came from that amounted to boxing your mother. On the other hand, he said, if Rosie cared to compete with him in any other sport, he would be glad to oblige her. Rex was a very calm and courteous conversationalist. He had poise. It was unconscious of course, but he had it just the same. He was just naturally a man who couldn't be hurried, flustered, or excited.

So Rex and Rosie fought it out in this game Leapfrog. They got to leaping over one another, quickly, too, until the first thing we knew the whole gang of us was out on the State Highway going south towards Fowler. It was a very hot day. Rosie and Rex were in great shape, and it looked like one was tougher than the other and more stubborn. They talked a good deal, especially Rosie, who insisted that she would have to fall down unconscious before she'd give up to a guy like Rex.

He said he was sorry his opponent was a girl. It grieved him deeply to have to make a girl exert herself to the point of death, but it was just too bad. He had to, so he had to. They leaped and squatted, leaped and squatted, and we got out to Sam Day's vineyard. That was half-way to Fowler. It didn't seem like either Rosie or Rex were ever going to get tired. They hadn't even begun to show signs of growing tired, although each of them was sweating a great deal.

Naturally, we were sure Rex would win the contest. But that was because we hadn't taken into account the fact that he was a simple person, whereas Rosie was crafty and shrewd. Rosie knew how to figure angles. She had discovered how to jump over Rex Folger in a way that weakened him. And after a while, about three miles out of Fowler, we noticed that she was coming down on Rex's *neck*, instead of on his back. Naturally, this was hurting him and making the blood rush to his head. Rosie herself squatted in such a way that it was impossible, almost, for Rex to get anywhere near her neck with his hands.

Before long, we noticed that Rex was weakening. His head was getting closer and closer to the ground. About half a mile out of Fowler, we heard Rex's head bumping the ground every time Rosie leaped over him. They were good loud bumps that we knew were painful, but Rex wasn't complaining. He was too proud to complain.

Rosie, on the other hand, knew she had her man, and she was giving him all she had. She was bumping his head on the ground as solidly as she could, because she knew she didn't have much more fight in her, and if she didn't lay him out cold, in the hot sun, in the next ten minutes or so, she would fall down exhausted herself, and lose the contest.

Suddenly Rosie bumped Rex's head a real powerful one. He got up very dazed and very angry. It was the first time we had ever seen him fuming. By God, the girl was taking advantage of him, if he wasn't mistaken, and he didn't like it. Rosie was squatted in front of him. He came up groggy and paused a moment. Then he gave Rosie a very effective kick that sent her sprawling. Rosie jumped up and smacked Rex in the mouth. The gang jumped in and tried to establish order.

It was agreed that the Leapfrog contest must not change into a fight. Not any more. Not with Fowler only five or ten minutes away. The gang ruled further that Rex had had no right to kick Rosie and that in smacking him in the mouth Rosie had squared the matter, and the contest was to continue.

Rosie was very tired and sore; and so was Rex. They began leaping and squatting again; and again we saw Rosie coming down on Rex's neck so that his head was bumping the ground.

It looked pretty bad for the boy from Texas. We couldn't understand how he could take so much punishment. We all felt that Rex was getting what he had coming to him, but at the same time everybody seemed to feel badly about Rosie, a girl, doing the job instead of one of us. Of course, that was where we were wrong. Nobody but Rosie could have figured out that smart way of humiliating a very powerful and superior boy. It was probably the woman in her, which, less than five years later, came out to such an extent that she became one of the most beautiful girls in town, gave up tomboy activities and married one of the wealthiest young men in Kings County, a college man named, if memory serves, Wallace Hadington Finlay VI.

Less than a hundred yards from the heart of Fowler, Rosie, with great and admirable artistry, finished the job.

That was where the dirt of the highway siding ended and the paved main street of Fowler began. This street was paved with cement, not asphalt. Asphalt, in that heat, would have been too soft to serve, but cement had exactly the right degree of brittleness. I think Rex when he squatted over the hard cement, knew the game was up. But he was brave to the end. He squatted over the hard cement and waited for the worst. Behind him, Rosie Mahoney prepared to make the supreme effort. In this next leap, she intended to give her all, which she did.

She came down on Rex Folger's neck like a ton of bricks. His head banged against the hard cement, his body straightened out, and his arms and legs twitched.

He was out like a light.

Six paces in front of him, Rosie Mahoney squatted and waited. Jim Telesco counted twenty, which was the time allowed for each leap. Rex didn't get up during the count.

The contest was over. The winner of the contest was Rosie Mahoney.

Rex didn't get up by himself at all. He just stayed where he was until a half-dozen of us lifted him and carried him to a horse trough, where we splashed water on his face.

Rex was a confused young man all the way back. He was also a deeply humiliated one. He couldn't understand anything about anything. He just looked dazed and speechless. Every now and then we imagined he wanted to talk, and I guess he did, but after we'd all gotten ready to hear what he had to say, he couldn't speak. He made a gesture so tragic that tears came to the eyes of eleven members of the gang.

Rosie Mahoney, on the other hand, talked all the way home. She said everything.

I think it made a better man of Rex. More human. After that he was a gentler sort of soul. It may have been because he couldn't see very well for some time. At any rate, for weeks he seemed to be going around in a dream. His gaze would freeze on some insignificant object far away on the landscape, and half the time it seemed as if he didn't know where he was going, or why. He took little part in the activities of the gang, and the following winter he stayed away altogether. He came to school one day wearing glasses. He looked broken and pathetic.

That winter Rosie Mahoney stopped hanging around with the gang, too. She had a flair for making an exit at the right time.

From *The Insurance Salesman and Other Stories* by WILLIAM SAROYAN

For discussion

Do you think this might be a true story? Do you know anyone like Rosie?

Do you sometimes find yourself involved in rivalries between girls and boys? Describe some of them.

Are you on Rosie's side, or Rex's, in this contest? Why?

Have you ever been speechless at something that has happened to you? Have you felt, like Rex, that no words can come anywhere near to what you feel? Describe what happened.

Why do you think the writer says it made a better man of Rex *and not a better* boy*?*

Rosie soon joined the gang in the district her parents moved to. Is it easy to make new friends when you move house? How have you made new friends?

Rosie changes too after the contest. In less than five years' time she became one of the most beautiful girls in the town. Do you know anyone who has changed? An older sister or brother, or cousin?

Do you expect to be the same or different, in five years' time?

On the next page is a piece about a boy getting to know some other children.

The Boys Next Door

Almost every afternoon three boys came out to play in the yard. They were all dressed alike, in grey coats and trousers, and identical caps; and all were round-cheeked and so closely resembled each other that I, watching them through a crack in the fence, could tell them apart only by their height. I looked on, unseen, but yearning to make them aware, in some way, of my presence. Their games were unfamiliar to me, but I liked them for the gay and amiable spirit in which they were played. Their clothes seemed attractive to me, too, and I admired them for their consideration toward each other, particularly marked in the attitude of the older boys to the youngest, a lively, comical little chap. They laughed at his falls—it being a universal reaction to laugh at anyone who trips—but there was no gloating in the laughter and they hurried over to help him up; and if he had soiled his hands or knees they wiped him off with their handkerchiefs or leaves, and the middle-sized boy would scold, good-naturedly, 'Now, clumsy!' I never saw them wrangle or take advantage of each other. They were all strong lads, nimble and tireless.

Climbing up a tree one day, I whistled to them. They stopped, looked at me, then came together in a huddle. Imagining that they were going to stone me, I dropped down for ammunition. With my pockets and the front of my blouse bulging with stones, I climbed back to my perch, but they had gone off to a far corner of the yard, where they played as if they had forgotten I was there. This experience ended in two disappointments; I didn't want to be the one to start a fight with them; and at that moment they were summoned from a window, 'Time to come in now, children.' And obediently, but unhurried, they went in, one behind the other, like geese.

Again and again I took that post in the tree overhanging the fence, in the hope that they would invite me to play with them; but the invitation never came. In my mind, however, I always joined in their games, and with such absorption that I would sometimes laugh or cry out, and that would again, after a look at me, bring them together in a huddle, while I, embarrassed, would scramble down and out of sight.

the oldest laughed at them, 'Fairy tales! We know all about that!'

But the others listened, absorbed; the smallest one with pursed lips, the middle one with his elbows on his knees, holding his brother's hand which was around his shoulder.

Evening was approaching, and the clouds over the roof had turned red, when suddenly the old man with the spiky moustache stood beside us. His cinnamon-coloured cloak was long, like a priest's, and he had on a shaggy fur cap.

'And who may he be?' he asked, pointing at me.

The oldest boy, standing up, nodded towards grandpa's house, 'He's from there.'

'Who invited him?'

The boys climbed down the sleigh, in silence, and trooped into their house, giving me a still stronger impression of a flock of geese.

With a hand that closed on my shoulder like a vice, the old man gripped me and pushed me before him, over the yard to the gate. I would have cried out in terror but his strides were so long and rapid, that before an outcry could escape from me, I was out in the street and he was standing at the gate, shaking a warning finger at me, 'Don't you ever come near me again!'

Enraged, myself, I shouted, 'I never wanted to come near you, you old devil!'

Once more the long arm shot out and I was hauled over the pavement, while his voice struck like a hammer on my skull, 'Is your grandfather home?'

Unluckily for me, he was; and with his head back and his beard projecting outward he looked into the bulbous dim, fish-eyes of the menacing old man, and explained, agitatedly, 'You see, his mother's away; and I'm busy, and there's nobody to see what he's up to; won't you overlook it this time, Colonel?'

The colonel paced about the room, raving like a lunatic. Then, almost before he was gone, I had got my beating.

Yet this dangerous acquaintance with the boys prospered and gave me increasing gratification. There was a little winding footpath between our house and the Ovsianikovs' fence. It was overgrown with elms, linden trees and elderberry bushes. Under their shade, as cover, I cut a hole through the fence; and the brothers visited me in turn, or sometimes two at a time. Crouched about that hole we held long conversations, in muted voices, while one of the brothers kept watch to prevent our being surprised by the colonel.

I learned what a miserable existence they led, and was sorry for them. We talked about my caged birds, and other boys' concerns, but I do not recall hearing a word from them about their father or stepmother. More often than not they wanted a story, and, as precisely as I could, I repeated grandma's; and if I was uncertain about a detail, I had them wait, while I went to her to get it right. Grandma was always pleased.

They heard much from me about grandma, and once the oldest brother commented, with an envious sigh, 'It seems your grandmother is good in every way. We used to have a good grandmother, too.'

From *My Childhood* by MAXIM GORKI

How are friendships with younger children different from friendships with people of your own age?

Do you find your friends because they live near you, or because they like doing the things you like doing? Or is there something else that makes you like them?

Have you anyone you would call a 'friend' among the grown-ups you know? Would you call Maxim Gorky's grandmother a friend to him?

Stepmothers are usually unpleasant or even wicked in stories. Are they like this in life?

Here is a poem about a boy at the exciting beginning stage of a friendship with a particular girl.

A Girl called Betty

I know a girl called Betty,
She was waiting down the road,
For me! for me! for me!
I wonder why I said,
'I would dread
To go with her.'
I wonder why.

DAVID *aged* 13

How do friendships grow and change?

Friendships between people of your own age, between boys and girls, and between children and older people, are all different; but how different, and in what ways?

When you feel yourself growing apart from a friend, how do you deal with it?

Friends can quarrel and we can hate them as easily as we love them.

Here are three *unfriendly* poems, all written by children at school.

It is impossible
for anyone to enter
our small world.
The adults don't
understand us
they think
we're childish.
No one can get in
our world.
It has a wall twenty feet high
and adults
have only ten feet ladders.

ROSS *aged* 11

When I look at my elders
I see them all as birds,—
The larks who like a song
And sing to their admirers,
The hawks who pounce on
The small and helpless.
The high hoverers
That look down from their lofty seat
But take no part
In what they see.
Those that flash their
Colourful plumage.
I see also they turn away
From the ungainly flight
Of some.

RICHARD *aged* 13

My Cousin

I remember my first enemy.
The pert, provoking child they said was my cousin.
I remember despising her straight limp hair,
The green glowering eyes,
And her slight lively body.
And that she despised my fluffy brown curls,
Pink complexion,
And plumpness.
They made us learn to dance together.
She was clumsy,
Her mouth pouted when she danced
But she said I was too fat to dance.
I wasn't.
They made us walk to school together.
She didn't even know her tables.
She couldn't knit.
I could knit when I was five,
But she laughed at me.
At home they made us play together:
She prodded me with bony fingers,
She pushed me down the stairs.
And when I saw her laughing
I screamed, until she cried.
I remember how I hated my cousin.

ROSALIND

For writing

Choose your own subject arising from reading and talking about these passages.

A continuation of the story of Rosie after she left the gang.

How you made a friend or lost a friend.

The odd man out.

If you could choose, would you prefer to be the oldest, the youngest or a middle one in a family?

Children in our street.

An account of a person you admire (any age).

Cousins.

The story of a grievous loss.

My sister's friends.

Old friends and new friends.

Older sisters: tyrants and protectors!

Yourself or one of your friends as you expect them to be in five years' time.

A story called 'An Act of Friendship'.

'She's my best friend and I hate her'.

A story called 'Breaking it up'.

Here is what an 11-year-old boy wrote about his hide-out, a special bit of his world.

My Hide-out

My hide-out is on the crumbles, to get there you walk down Fort Road and keep on until you have passed three iron posts. When you come to the fourth post you walk straight to the left (inland). The first thing you will see is a flight of steps leading to an underground room. If you go there you will have to take a light for the room is very dark. If you are followed, there are some holes in the ground, so you can hide in them. Usually I go with my cousin. We take some cards and have a game with them, it is fun to sit in the candle light and watch shadows dancing round. The hide-out is not very far from the sea and you can get to the beach in about three minutes. I go to the hide-out nearly every Saturday sometime my grandad comes with me. The place makes a super place for playing cowboys. On Saturdays when you are on the beach and it rains the hide-out is a place you can shelter in. Because the hide-out is water tight. In the back of the room is a hole where you can hide things, the hole can easily be blocked up with a piece of cork. You cannot see the place from Fort Road because a big hill of stones hide it. There is an old track of grass and moss leading to the hide-out. My grandad said it was made by soldiers of long ago so they could pull a heavy cart along without making a noise on the stones. The wall along the hide-out is about a quarter of a mile long and at one end there is a concrete platform for a cannon to stand on.

ALAN

Discussion

What do you think of this?

There are many things to discuss about it, for instance: does it make you feel you would like to see it? Does it give you a clear picture of what it is like and where it is situated? Could you find it on your own, or doesn't this matter? Has he told us all we want to know about it?

Proof-correcting exercise

This piece of writing has been printed just as Alan wrote it and he has forgotten to put in some of his punctuation marks. Before a piece of writing is printed, the author usually makes sure that it is correct. The printer sets it up in type and shows the author roughly printed sheets—the proofs. Then the author has a second chance to correct mistakes before his work is printed. In Appendix I you will find the special signs that should be used in correcting a manuscript for the printer. You will also find there a piece of writing by a boy of 11 corrected for printing in the proper way by using these signs. *Use these signs in correcting a manuscript, either your own last piece or* 'My Hide-out'.

Most children have some secret place of their own. This one was on the seashore; sometimes they are in trees or under bushes, and city children often find special places of their own too.

Can you do as well, or better than Alan on the subject: 'A secret place of my own.'

Another Hide-out

This passage comes from *The Adventures of Huckleberry Finn* which is about a wild American boy who runs away from his drunken father in the company of Jim, a Negro. They have many adventures on their journey down the great Mississippi river. This passage describes their hide-out on the raft drifting fast down the river, but in the third and fourth paragraphs Huck tells us some things that Alan doesn't mention in his account of his hide-out.

When the first streak of day began to show, we tied up to a tow-head in a big bend in the Illinois side, and hacked off cotton-wood branches with the hachet and covered up the raft with them so she looked like there had been a cave-in in the bank there. A tow-head is a sand-bar that has cotton woods on it....

When it was beginning to come on dark, we poked our heads out of the cotton-wood thicket and looked up, and down, and across; nothing in sight; so Jim took up some of the top planks of the raft and built a snug wigwam to get under in blazing weather and rainy, and to keep the things dry. Jim made a floor for the wigwam, and raised it a foot or more above the level of the raft, so now the blankets and all the traps was out of the reach of steamboat waves. Right in the middle of the wigwam we made a layer of dirt about five or six inches deep with a frame around it to hold it to its place; this was to built a fire on in sloppy weather or chilly; the wigwam would keep it from being seen. We made an extra steering oar too, because one of the others might get broke, on a snag or something. We fixed up a short forked stick to hang the old lantern on; because we must always light the lantern whenever we see a steamboat coming down-stream, to keep from getting run over....

This second night we run between seven and eight hours, with a current that was making over four miles an hour. We catched fish, and talked, and took a swim now and then to keep off sleepiness. It was kind of solemn, drifting down the big still river, laying on our backs looking up at the stars, and we didn't ever feel like talking loud, and it warn't often that we laughed, only a little kind of low chuckle. We had mighty good weather, as a general thing, and nothing ever happened to us at all, that night, nor the next, nor the next.

Every night we passed towns, some of them away up on black hillsides, nothing but just a shiney bed of lights, not a house could you see. The fifth night we passed St. Louis, and it was like the whole world lit up. . . . They used to say there was twenty or thirty thousand people in St. Louis, but I never believed it till I see that wonderful spread of lights at two o'clock that still night. There warn't a sound there; everybody was asleep.

The Adventures of Huckleberry Finn by MARK TWAIN

Discussion

What kind of things does Huck tell us which Alan doesn't mention? Look at the third paragraph in particular. Why do you think they felt 'kind of solemn'?

What do you think of Huck's English?

There is a lot here which your teachers would ask you to correct if you wrote like this, yet Mark Twain wrote his book exactly as it is printed here, and the printer did not consider it necessary to correct it. Why was this, do you think?

Exercise and discussion

Try rewriting the third or fourth paragraph and correcting anything that seems to you not to be good English; then read your version aloud followed by the original one and discuss whether you have improved it or made it worse.

Do you think any parts of it are particularly good? Are there any parts of your own piece which are particularly good? When you have sorted out your ideas about how good (or bad) this language is, take another look at Alan's piece and see if you have any further ideas about what is good or bad about it.

Now for your friends and the things you do together

Here is a passage from a story about four boys who go off camping together one summer holiday.

Leading down from the gate, there was a lane to the first beach. It was high tide, and we heard the sea dashing. Four boys on a roof of a lorry—one tall, dark, regular-featured, precise of speech, in a good suit, a boy of the world; one squat, ungainly, red-haired, his red wrists fighting out of short, frayed sleeves; one heavily spectacled, small-paunched, with indoor shoulders and feet in always unlaced boots wanting to go different ways; one small, thin, indecisively active, quick to get dirty, curly—saw their field in front of them, a fortnight's new home that had thick, pricking hedges for walls, the sea for a front garden, a green gutter for a lavatory and a wind-struck tree in the very middle.

I helped Dan unload the lorry while Sidney tipped the driver and George struggled with the farm-yard gate and looked at the ducks inside. The lorry drove away.

'Let's build our tents by the tree in the middle', said George.

'Pitch!' Sidney said, unlatching the gate for him.

We pitched our tents in a corner, out of the wind.

'One of us must light the primus', Sidney said, and, after George had burned his hand, we sat in a circle outside the sleeping-tent talking about motor-cars, content to be in the country, lazily easy in each other's company, thinking to ourselves as we talked, knowing always that the sea dashed on the rocks not far below us and rolled out into the world, and that tomorrow we would bathe and throw a ball on the sands and stone a bottle on a rock and perhaps meet three girls. The oldest would be for Sidney, the plainest for Dan, and the youngest for me. George broke his spectacles when he spoke to girls; he had to walk off, blind as a bat, and the next morning he would say: 'I'm sorry I had to leave you, but I remembered a message'.

It was past five o'clock. My father and mother would have finished tea; the plates with famous castles on them were cleared from the table; father with a newspaper, mother with socks, were far away in the blue haze to the left, up a hill, in a villa, hearing from the park the faint cries of children drift over the public tennis courts, and wondering where I was and what I was doing. I was alone with my friends in a field, with a blade of grass in my mouth saying 'Dempsey would hit him cold', and thinking of the great whale . . . thrashing on the top of the sea, or plunging underneath, like a mountain.

'Bet you I can beat you to the end of the field'.

Dan and I raced among the cowpads, George thumping on our heels.

'Let's go down to the beach'.

Sidney led the way, running straight as a soldier in his khaki shorts, over a stile, down fields to another, into a wooded valley, up through heather on to a clearing near the edge of a cliff, where two broad boys were wrestling outside a tent. I saw one bite the other in the leg, they both struck expertly and savagely at the face, one struggled clear, and with a leap, the other had him face to the ground. They were Brazell and Skully.

'Hallo, Brazell and Skully!' said Dan.

Skully had Brazell's arm in a policeman's grip; he gave it two quick twists and stood up, smiling.

'Hallo, boys! Hallo, Little Cough! How's your father?'

'He's very well, thank you.'

Brazell, on the grass, felt for broken bones. 'Hallo, boys! How are your fathers?'

They were the worst and biggest boys in school. Every day for a term they caught me before class began and wedged me in the waste-paper basket and then put the basket on the master's desk. Sometimes I could get out and sometimes not. Brazell was lean, Skully was fat.

From *Portrait of the Artist as a Young Dog* by DYLAN THOMAS

This writer, Dylan Thomas, takes you right into his small gang of friends and into their camp site on the Welsh coast. He also takes you into their heads and tells you what they are thinking about and planning to do, as well as what they actually do, and lets you feel their alarm when they find their enemies from their school camping so near them. Moreover, not everything we are told about happens in this place at this time. We flash back and forward in Dylan's mind between his home—without him—and later to his school.

We Play Games

The hunt was over. A rug was spread in the shade of some young birch-trees and the whole company disposed themselves in a circle on the rug. Gavrilo, the butler, having stamped down the lush green grass around him, was wiping plates and taking out of the box plums and peaches wrapped in leaves. The sun shone through the green branches of the young birches and cast round, quivering medallions of light on the pattern of the rug, on my legs and even on Gavrilo's perspiring bald head.

When we had our share of ice-cream and fruit it was no use sitting on the rug any longer so in spite of the scorching of the oblique rays of the sun we got up and proceeded to play games.

'Well, what shall it be?' said Lyuba, screwing her eyes up in the sun and hopping about on the grass. 'Let's play Robinson!'

'No . . . that's too dull,' said Volodya, sprawling on the grass and chewing some leaves. 'It's always Robinson! If you must do something, we'd better build a summer-house.'

Volodya was obviously putting on airs; probably he was proud of having ridden the hunter and was pretending to be very tired. Or perhaps even at that age he was too matter-of-fact and had too little imagination really to enjoy playing at Robinson, which consisted in performing scenes from *The Swiss Family Robinson* which we had read not long before.

'Please do . . . why won't you do what we want?' the girls insisted. 'You can be Charles, or Ernest, or the father, whichever you like,' said Katya, trying to pull him up from the ground by the sleeve of his jacket.

'I really don't want to—it's a silly game!' said Volodya, stretching himself and at the same time smiling smugly.

'It would have been better to stay at home if no one wants to play,' declared Lyuba in tears.

She was an awful cry-baby.

'All right, come along then; only please don't cry. I can't stand it!'

Volodya's condescension afforded us very little satisfaction; on the contrary his lazy bored look destroyed all the fun of the game. When we sat on the ground, and pretended we were going fishing, began to row with all our might, Volodya sat with folded arms in an attitude which had nothing in common with the attitude of a fisherman. I told him so but he retorted that by waving our arms about more vigorously or less we should not gain or lose anything, and should not travel any the further. I could not help agreeing with him. When I pretended to go hunting and set off into the woods with a stick over my shoulder Volodya lay down on his back with his hands behind his head and told me he would pretend to be coming too. Such talk and behaviour had a damping effect on the game and were extremely distasteful, the more so because in one's secret heart one had to admit that Volodya was right.

I knew myself that not only could I not kill a bird with a stick but that I could not even make it fire. It was just a game. Once you begin arguing like that it becomes equally impossible to ride out for a drive on chairs; and, I thought, Volodya must remember how in the long winter evenings we covered an arm-chair with a shawl to turn it into a carriage. One of us sat in front as the coachman, someone else was a footman, and the girls sat in the middle. Three chairs were the horses—and we were off. And what adventures we used to meet on the way, and how gaily and swiftly those winter evenings passed. . . . If you only go by what's real there won't be any games. And if there are no games, what is left?

From *Childhood, Boyhood, Youth* by LEO TOLSTOY

For writing and discussion

Friends, special places, and things you like to do with your friends. . . .

Write a story about two or three friends who find a place they decide to make their particular rendezvous.

Write a further story about some of the things they did together from this 'Headquarters'.

Why do you think Brazell and Skully were enemies? Write about an occasion when you encountered an enemy.

Choose some part of the world that interests you, and that you know something about from Geography lessons or watching TV, and write a story about yourself and your companions and an adventure you had there – in Alaska, the Antarctic, the Amazon forests, the Canadian Rocky Mountains, for instance.

You might re-read the account of Huck Finn travelling down the Mississippi on the raft or find some books from the library about the area you are interested in.

A mysterious encounter: man or beast?

Robert Louis Stevenson wrote a story called Dr. Jekyll and Mr. Hyde. *Dr. Jekyll and Mr. Hyde were, in fact, the same person. He lived two quite different lives, a villain in one and an ordinary sort of person in the other. He changed his whole appearance and personality and behaviour as he shifted from one life to the other. In the end his two personalities began to war with each other and he died in the 'battle'.*

Write a story in which you or someone you know leads a double life. Did they have different sets of friends? What kind of places did the two 'halves' do things in, and what kind of adventures did they have?

This might turn into a long story of three or four chapters.

Sometimes you want to be a child and do things and play games that you know only children would play; at other times you do things when you really need to be as much like grown-ups as you can be. Re-read the stories of Huck Finn and Dylan Thomas going camping and discuss whether they were being children or grown-ups.

Write about an occasion when you felt you were enjoying doing what only children do, or

Write about an occasion when you needed to be as grown-up as you could manage.

Read the section in Chief Plenty-coups's autobiography about his memories of play when he was a child (p. 152). Was it different or similar to how you play? Do you think grown-ups play?

Write about a butterfly, or a cat, or a seal, or any animal whose powers you would like to possess.

Re-read the story 'We Play Games' on p. 31.

Whose side are you on in the argument about what they should do?

Write about any make-believe character who was once very real for you.

Write a story about a toy that came alive.

Write a story called 'I play at being someone else'.

Do you like acting?

Write a story about being a character in a play, and how when the play was over you found you had turned into the character you were impersonating. What happened when you got home?

Waiting for the Bus

Under the glaring lamp we wait,
A chattering crowd of girls,
Sucking refreshers and aniseed balls,
Shrouded in brown gaberdines.

Cold and clammy the fog surrounds us,
Makes us shiver and stamp our feet
On the wet grimy pavement that glistens with light,
And splash through the muddy brown pools.

Satchels under our arms, we gossip
Of teachers, of homework, of friends,
And lean on the grey concrete shelter
And wait for the 209.

Then out of the sleet and the fog we hear
The engine's rumble and grunt,
And lighted windows are golden and warm,
And the glass is steamy with heat.

We rush through the mud to the throbbing red bus,
And leap on, and struggle, and push,
And charge up the stairs, and flop down on the seat,
And we're cheerful, and crowded, and warm.

CELIA

2. Home and Family

Family photograph albums (or boxes of colour transparencies) are full of snapshots of brothers and sisters, parents, uncles and aunts, grandparents, pets, picnics and places we have enjoyed going to. But a photograph tells you very little compared with a piece of writing. Some boys and girls in a London school each made albums of a different sort. They were all called 'My Home and Family', and contained many snapshots but they were arranged so that there was only one picture on each left-hand page. On the right-hand pages were written pieces which went with the picture on the page opposite. One book had a photograph of a boy by himself in a garden; underneath was written 'Peter'. The writing on the opposite page was headed 'Only child'. The photograph showed what Peter looked like but the writing told what it felt like to be an only child. Another photograph was called 'Myself'. Here is what was written on the opposite page:

Myself

I must introduce myself. I am a girl of twelve years old and I am labelled Anna. I live in London much to my disgust.

I don't know why, but when you want something an awful lot you can't have it. What I want is a cat or a dog, but I live in the sort of house where you can't keep one.

There is another thing that I want, but I can only dream of it, and that is to go to a Drama School.

These are my two main dreams, although I have many others.

You must not think that my life is full of dreams. There are a lot of things that I do and like doing very much such as riding my bicycle, reading any book I like, going camping and going on holiday by myself.

Oh no! Don't get the impression that I don't like my family. I do, it's just that I like being by myself. Then I can do all the things that I like, well, not all, but I can think for a nice long time.

Now I must tell you of something that has invaded my life—'THEM'. I don't know what 'THEM' are exactly but they make me do certain things and they hide and follow me, especially when it's dark. If I do something which isn't to their liking they might kill me.

For instance, if I am running along in a certain road and I get tired of it I must do it for eleven more steps. If I don't THEY will make something terrible happen to me. If I am counting blackbirds I must count eleven more before I stop counting them.

Walking outside at night I can often feel them watching me, waiting for me to do something wrong. My one comfort against THEM is that other people have THEM.

Besides liking, wishing, disliking, and THEM, looking forward to plays is a great part of my life. At the moment I am looking forward to my first holiday abroad. But before that there are four horrid weeks of school.

ANNA

Discussion

What do you think of Anna's piece? She tells us the things she finds most interesting about herself. What do you like, wish for, dislike, dread, and look forward to?

What do you think of the way Anna has paragraphed her pieces? Are there too many paragraphs, or do you think it is just right?

For writing

Some of the other snapshots in the books had these captions under them:

Dad.
My elder brother.
The oldest member of our family.
Our house.
The twins.
Our youngest.
My dog (cat, tortoise, hamster, budgerigar, etc.).
My uncle.

Choose one of these, or some other, and write the piece that is to go on the page opposite the picture in order to fill in something of what the photograph does not tell. Or you may like to start making a similar book of your home and family.

The following piece was written by an African girl whose home was in the interior of Uganda. Her native language is called LUGANDA which is spoken by the people of BUGANDA who are known as THE BAGANDA, a tribe in UGANDA. She had been learning English for about five years at school.

My Aunt

My Aunt is a big, good looking woman with pigs' eyes. She is short and fat and her feet—oh like elephant's feet. She has not much hair. Her head looks like the hippopotamus's skin. She always looks as though she has lost something very expensive. She looks as if she is crying. She looks so dull and she speaks stiffly. She never takes any notice of anybody who comes to see her.

She loves only my father who is her brother. Her voice sounds like the voice of a little girl of eight years. She walks slowly like ducks floating on the sea, and she sometimes knocks her feet against stones. And she is rather greedy for she hates cooking food for her visitors. She hates visitors since she lost her husband and her children.

She sleeps in a big house alone and she hates us. Her manners are very bad.

SARAH KIRONDE. *Secondary School*, Kampala

Discussion

How might you have guessed that this was written by an African girl?

Could you do as well in French?

For writing

Look up 'Uganda' in an encyclopedia or a good geography book and write a story about this part of Africa.

In another part of Africa, the Cameroons, there is a village school where the children live for the term as their homes are too far away for them to go each day. Here they have made some of their own textbooks with the help of their teacher. The language they are learning is French so they exchange letters with the children in a small village in southern France, and out of these letters the book was made. Here is what an African boy called Bouba and a French boy called Jacques wrote about their homes. Although the pieces are short, they are vivid and exact, so that the reader knows what their homes looked like, what they were built of, and what the surrounding countryside was like. Furthermore, Bouba tells us how he feels about his home—but as he has been away from it for a term, perhaps we should expect him to put this in his letter.

BOUBA AND JACQUES: THE BIRTH OF A DIALOGUE BETWEEN AFRICA AND EUROPE

This is my Home

BOUBA

In June, when the school closes I shall walk down the hill towards my village, very happy to see my home again.

All around it are young cotton plants, corn and millet. It has a straw roof which keeps it fresh and cool. The side which looks out on the road has a verandah. The second side has a window but as it is unprotected, it is always drenched during the rainy season. The third side also has a verandah held up by two open brick walls. This is where my father quietly sits sewing his clothes. We also eat our meals there and sleep out at night during the hot season.

I shall be glad to sleep in the house where I was born.

JACQUES

My home seems to hang on a red and green hillside: brick-red soil and green alfalfa and young corn. The house is built of stone covered by rough-cast plaster. The walls are pink and the tiled roof is covered with moss. Some grey and white pigeons circle overhead and with a fluttering of wings land on the stone-edged pigeon-house.

In another building on the far side of the stone courtyard are the barn, the sheep-pen, the stable and the pigsty.

In an open shed leaning against a wall my father keeps his cart and his binder. In the same shed is the sling in which we put the oxen when it is being shod.

When they had written about their homes and parents and relations and animals, they went on to write about some of the things they did. The following pieces describe how they 'helped' their parents. It is called 'The Day we were Herdsmen'. Both were only partially successful and their feelings about their day's 'work' were rather mixed.

The Day we were Herdsmen

BOUBA

My father calls me. 'Go into the hut and take down the stick and the gourd that are hanging from the roof, he says. 'Now go after your big brother', he tells me, 'you are going to look after the herd'.

I am pleased at the idea of looking after the animals. With the gourd in my hand and the stick over my shoulder I run after my brother and take his place. At the water's edge our beasts drink their fill. I cut a stem of wild millet and make a little flute. While the goats are nibbling at the young grass, I join the other little herdsmen, who are also busy making flutes. We blow our flutes together and make some fine tunes.

Then we send the smallest children back to the village. 'You, Oumarou, bring us some millet flour, and you, Djibrilla, some dried fish'. We do our cooking and drink the water in our gourds. In the evening we sing as we go home.

JACQUES

Julien and I have been told to watch over the oxen. We leave them to graze and run to the cherry tree. Julien climbs it, cuts off branches loaded with cherries and throws them to me. We eat lots of cherries and we even swallow the stones.

An hour goes by and Julien comes down from the tree. When we go back to the field the oxen have disappeared. We look for them in the other fields and finally go back to the village.

Father is waiting for us on the stairs. 'The oxen came back on their own at full gallop', he tells us severely.

We feel vexed and foolish. We hardly eat any supper and we don't sleep much that night—we both have stomach ache.

From *Unesco Courier*

Discussion

Most children have work that they do at home or outside school. Some look after younger children, some do the shopping on Saturdays, some do a paper round, some clean cars, and country children often have responsible work to do with the farm animals or in the fields at harvest time.

What jobs have you done? Which do you like, and dislike? What difficulties did you find? Are there any jobs you think you can do better than grown-ups?

For writing

Whether you have any foreign pen-friends or not you could make an interesting book about your homes, parents, relatives, animals, and the things you do. Here are some of the titles that Bouba and Jacques used in their book; you could make any new ones that you wanted:

This is my home.
My father.
Harvest time.
The day we were herdsmen.
Night fishing.
Magic riders and cyclists.
When I grow up.

If you live in a city or town, some of your titles might include:

A wedding in our road.
The street market.
Shopping expedition.
Saturday afternoon in the park.
Railway station.
Staying out late in the city.

When children are very small (between 2 and 3 years old) they often talk or chant to themselves. Here is what a toddler of $2\frac{1}{2}$ sang to herself in bed at night.

My home is at Belstone.
I don't know where it is, Belstone.
We can't see Belstone from here.
We couldn't go down there, could we?
No, we couldn't.

What does 'home' mean to you?

Is it the house you live in? or the place where the house is? or is it where your parents live (even a tent or a caravan)? Do you think gypsies, or nomadic people like some of the Arabs use a word meaning 'home'? If you live with foster parents or relatives do you think of this as home? Or is it perhaps where you feel secure and can meet your friends?

Write a monologue (a speech to yourself) in which you ask yourself and answer to yourself questions about Home.

Here is a story about a home and a family, four boys and three girls, Marjorie, Dorothy, Phyllis, Harold, Jack, Tony and I.

Read it aloud and talk about it, and talk about your own home and mother and father and brothers and sisters—and anyone else who lives in your home. Say what it looks like, and smells like, and sounds like, and how you feel about it at different times. And what jokes do you have? Laurie Lee says in his story that they had 'a sofa for cats and a harmonium for coats'.

The Kitchen

With our Mother, then, we made eight in that cottage and disposed of its three large floors. There was the huge white attic which ran the length of the house, where the girls slept on fat striped mattresses; an ancient, plaster-crumbling room whose sloping ceilings bulged like tent-cloths. The roof was so thin that rain and bats filtered through, and you could hear a bird land on the tiles. Mother and Tony shared a bedroom below; Jack, Harold and I the other.

But our waking life, and our growing years, were for the most part spent in the kitchen, and until we married, or ran away, it was the common room we shared. Here we lived and fed in a family fug, not minding the little space, trod on each other like birds in a hole, elbowed our ways without spite, all talking at once or all silent at once, or crying against each other, but never I think feeling overcrowded, being as separate as notes in a scale.

That kitchen, worn by our boots and lives, was scruffy, warm, and low, whose fuss of furniture seemed never the same but was shuffled around each day. A black grate crackled with coal and beech-twigs; towels toasted on the guard; the mantel was littered with fine old china, horse brasses, and freak potatoes. On the floor were strips of muddy matting, the windows were choked with plants, the walls supported stopped clocks and calendars, and smoky fungus ran over the ceilings. There were also six tables of different sizes, some armchairs gapingly stuffed, boxes, stools, and unravelling baskets, books and papers on every chair, a sofa for cats, a harmonium for coats, and a piano for dust and photographs.

The day was over and we had used it, running errands or prowling the fields. When evening came we returned to the kitchen, back to its smoky comfort, in from the rapidly cooling air to its wrappings of warmth and cooking. We boys came first, scuffling down the bank, singly, like homing crows.

Indoors, our mother was cooking pancakes, her face aglow from the fire. There was a smell of sharp lemon and salty batter, and a burning hiss of oil. The kitchen was dark and convulsive with shadows, no lights had yet been lit. Flames leapt, subsided, corners woke and died, fires burned in a thousand brasses.

'Poke round for the matches, dear boy,' said Mother. 'Damn me if I know where they got to.'

We lit the candles and set them about, each in its proper order: two on the mantelpiece, one on the piano, and one on a plate in the window.

Next we filled and lit the tall iron lamp and placed it on the table. When the wick had warmed and was drawing properly, we turned it up full strength. The flame in the funnel then sprang alive and rose like a pointed flower, began to sing and shudder and grow more radiant, throwing pools of light on the ceiling. Even so, the kitchen remained mostly in shadow, its walls a voluptuous gloom.

The time had come for my violin practice. I began twanging the strings with relish. Mother was still frying and rolling up pancakes; my brothers lowered their heads and sighed. I propped my music on the mantelpiece and sliced through a Russian Dance while sweet smells of resin mixed with lemon and fat as the dust flew in clouds from my bow. Now and then I got a note just right, and then Mother would throw me a glance. A glance of piercing, anxious encouragement as she side-stepped my swinging arm. Plump in her slippers, one hand to her cheek, her pan beating time in the other, her hair falling down about her ears, mouth working to help out the tune—old and tired though she was, her eyes were a girl's and it was for looks such as these that I played.

'Splendid!' she cried. 'Top-hole! Clap clap! Now give us another, me lad.'

So I slashed away at 'William Tell', and when I did that, plates jumped; and Mother skipped gaily around the hearthrug, and even Tony rocked a bit in his chair.

Meanwhile Jack had cleared some boots from the table and started his inscrutable homework. Tony, in his corner, began to talk to the cat and play with some fragments of cloth. So with the curtains drawn close and the pancakes coming, we settled down to the evening. When the kettle boiled and the toast was made, we gathered and had our tea. We grabbed and dodged and passed and snatched, and packed our mouths like pelicans.

Mother ate always standing up, tearing crusts off the loaf with her fingers, a hand-to-mouth feeding that expressed her vigilance, like that of a wireless-operator at sea. For most of Mother's attention was fixed on the grate, whose fire must never go out.

But tonight the firelight snapped and crackled, and Mother was in full control. She ruled the range and all its equipment with tireless, nervous touch. Eating with one hand, she threw on wood with the other, raked the ashes, and heated the oven, put on a kettle, stirred the pot, and spread out some more shirts on the guard. As soon as we boys had finished our tea; we pushed all the crockery aside, piled it up roughly at the far end of the table, and settled down under the lamp. Its light was warm and live around us, a kind of puddle of fire of its own. I set up my book and began to draw. Jack worked at his notes and figures. Tony was playing with some cotton reels, pushing them slowly round the table.

All was silent except for Tony's voice, softly muttering his cotton-reel story.

'. . . So they come out of this big hole see, and the big chap said Fie he said we'll kill 'em see, and the pirates was waiting up 'ere, and they had this gurt cannon and they went bang fire and the big chap fell down wheeee! and rolled back in the 'ole and I said we got 'em and I run up the 'ill and this boat see was comin' and I jumped on board wooosh crump and I said now I'm captain see and they said fie and I took me 'achet 'ack 'ack and they fell plop in the sea wallop and I sailed the boat round 'ere and round 'ere and up 'ere and round 'ere and down 'ere and up 'ere and round 'ere and down 'ere. . . .

Now the girls arrived home in their belted mackintoshes, flushed from their walk through the dark, and we looked up from our games and said; 'Got anything for us?' and Dorothy gave us some liquorice. Then they all had their supper at one end of the table while we boys carried on at the other. When supper was over and cleared away, the kitchen fitted us all. We drew together round the evening lamp, the vast and easy time. . . . Marjorie began to trim a new hat, Dorothy to write a love-letter, Phyllis sat down with some forks and spoons, blew ah! and sleepily rubbed them. Harold, home late, cleaned his bike in a corner. Mother was cutting up newspapers.

We talked in spurts, in lowered voices, scarcely noticing if anyone answered.

Marge gave her silky, remembering laugh and looked fondly across at Tony. The fire burned clear with a bottle-green light. Their voices grew low and furry. A farm-dog barked far across the valley, fixing the time and distance exactly. Warned by the dog and some hooting owls, I could sense the night valley emptying, stretching in mists of stars and water, growing slowly more secret and late.

From *Cider with Rosie* by LAURIE LEE

Here is a piece written by a girl of 11 called Grace. She lived in a big apartment block in New York City.

What a Block!

My block is the most terrible block I've ever seen. There are at least 25 or 30 narcotic people in my block. The cops come around there and try to act bad but I bet inside of them they are as scared as can be. They even had in the papers that this block is the worst block, not in Manhattan but in New York City. In the summer they don't do nothing except shooting, stabbing, and fighting. They hang all over the stoops[1] and when you say excuse me to them they hear you but they just don't feel like moving. Some times they make me so mad that I feel like slapping them and stuffing a bag of garbage down their throats. There's only one policeman who can handle these people and we all call him 'Sunny.' When he comes around in his cop car the people run around the corners, and he won't let anyone sit on the stoops. If you don't believe this story come around some time and you'll find out.

Suggestions for writing

Read the story called 'The Kitchen' on page 47.

Write a piece about your own home. Choose one particular time of day and try to get down all the things that happen and the way you feel about them.

[1] Stoops: balconies

Not all homes are happy. Sometimes children hate the places where they live.

If you live—or have ever lived—somewhere you disliked, write about it.

Write a piece in which you 'think on paper' about the mixture of liking and disliking, happiness and quarrels that make up 'home'.

Write a story called 'Leaving Home'.

Read the first three paragraphs of 'The Kitchen' again and write about a room you know well and use a lot. This kind of room is usually full of things that are part of what people do in the room, or things they have brought in because they are treasures, or things they have left there because they went off to do something else.

A story about family life. One of the following titles may give you a start:
Turning out old toys.
Visiting relations.
A homecoming.
A party.

A story about:
The attic.
The cellar.
The empty house.
Noises at night.
The day you got up very early.
A day at home.
The cat's view of life in your house.
An unexpected visitor.
The frog in the fridge.
Life in a caravan.
On the move.

3. School

In many American schools driving a car is one of the things all the pupils have to learn and in some Russian schools they can learn such things as computor programming, radio technology, practical printing, and many other things. In some British schools you can join classes in boat building, navigation and charting, playing the guitar and other instruments, practical dressmaking, and learning Chinese.

Make a list in two columns of the particular things you would like to learn to do, and the subjects you would like to study in your first year in Secondary School.

'Lessons with George' is about an English boy who was living on the Greek island of Corfu. There was no English school for him to go to and he could not go to a Greek school because he could not speak Greek. His mother decided he was getting wild so she arranged for a friend called George to come every day to teach him.

Lessons with George

George and I regarded each other with suspicion. He was a very tall and extremely thin man who moved with the odd disjointed grace of a puppet. His lean skull-like face was partially concealed by a finely pointed brown beard and a pair of large tortoise-shell spectacles. . . .

Gravely George set about the task of teaching me. He was undeterred by the fact that there were no school books available on the island; he simply ransacked his own library. . . . He taught me the rudiments of geography from the maps in the back of an ancient copy of *Pears Encyclopedia* and French from a fat and exciting book called *Le Petit Larousse*, and mathemathics from memory. From my point of view however, the most important thing was that we devoted some of our time to natural history, and George carefully taught me how to observe and how to note down observations in a diary. At once my enthusiastic but haphazard interest in nature became focused, for I found that by writing things down I could learn and remember much more. . . .

'Let me see, let me see,' George would murmur, running a long forefinger down our carefully prepared timetable; 'Yes, yes, mathematics. If I remember rightly we were involved in the Herculean task of discovering how long it would take six men to build a wall if three of them took a week. I seem to recall that we have spent almost as much time on this problem as the men spent on the wall . . . . Let us see if we can make it more exciting.

He would droop over the exercise book pensively, pulling at his beard. Then in his large clear writing he would set the problem out in a fresh way.

'If it took two caterpillars a week to eat eight leaves, how long would four caterpillars take to eat the same number? Now, apply yourself to that . . . .'

In geography we made better progress for George was able to give a more zoological tinge to the lessons. We would draw giant maps, wrinkled with mountains, and then fill in the various places of interest, together with drawings of the more exciting fauna to be found there. . . . Our maps were works of art. . . . Our brown sun-drenched deserts were lumpy with camel-humps and pyramids, and our tropical forests so tangled and luxuriant that it was only with difficulty that the slouching jaguars, lithe snakes, and morose gorillas managed to get through them. Our rivers were wide and blue as forget-me-nots, freckled with canoes and crocodiles. Our oceans were anything but empty. Whales allowed unseaworthy galleons to pursue them with a forest of harpoons, octopi engulfed small boats, Chinese junks were followed by shoals of sharks, fur-clad Eskimos pursued herds of walrus through ice-fields thickly populated by polar bears and penguins. They were maps that lived, maps one could study, frown over, and add to; maps, in short, that really *meant* something.

Our attempts at history were not, at first, conspicuously successful, until George discovered that by seasoning a series of unpalatable facts with a sprig of zoology and a sprinkle of completely irrelevant detail, he could get me interested. . . . Breathlessly, history lesson by history lesson, I followed Hannibal's progress over the Alps. His reason for attempting such a feat, and what he intended to do on the other side, were details that scarcely worried me. No, my interest in what I considered to be a very badly planned expedition lay in the fact that *I knew the name of each and every elephant*. I also knew that Hannibal had appointed a special man not only to feed and look after the elephants, *but to give them hot water bottles when the weather got cold*. . . . Another thing that most history books never seem to mention is that Columbus's first words on setting foot in America were: 'Great heavens, look . . . a jaguar!' . . . . So George, hampered by inadequate books and a reluctant pupil would strive to make his teaching interesting, so that the lessons did not drag.

From *My Family and Other Animals* by GERALD DURRELL.

For discussion and writing

This boy wasn't really interested in anything except natural history, but he knew a great deal about this. Have you any special interests that you know a lot about?

Have you ever tried to teach anyone anything—younger brothers or sisters for instance? Did they learn whatever it was you were teaching them?

Do you think George was a good teacher? Would you like to have lessons by yourself? What difference would it make?

Do you think your school is too big, or do you like being in a big school?

Do you like working on your own?

Who do you like discussing your work with—friends? teachers? parents? older pupils? Who do you get most help from in learning the things you want to learn?

In the next day or two note down some observations of anything or anyone you are interested in, and test George's theory that by writing things down you can learn and remember more. Is it true for you? You might observe babies, for instance, if there is one in your home, or little children—how they walk and speak and what they do. Or you may be more interested in animals, or motor cars, or streets, or trees . . . .

The Idealist

I don't know how it is about education, but it never seemed to do anything for me but get me into trouble.

Adventure stories weren't so bad, but as a kid I was very serious and preferred realism to romance. School stories were what I liked best, and, judged by our standards, these were romantic enough for anyone. The schools were English, so I suppose you couldn't expect anything else. They were always called 'the venerable pile', and there was usually a ghost in them; they were built in a square that was called 'the quad' and, according to the pictures, they were all clock-towers, spires, and pinnacles, like the lunatic asylum with us. The fellows in the stories were all good climbers, and got in and out of school at night on ropes made of knotted sheets. They dressed queerly; they wore long trousers, short, black jackets, and top hats. Whenever they did anything wrong they were given 'lines' in Latin. When it was a bad case, they were flogged and never showed any sign of pain; only the bad fellows, and they always said: 'Ow Ow!'

Most of them were grand chaps who always stuck together and were great at football and cricket. They never told lies and wouldn't talk to anyone who did. If they were caught out and asked a point-blank question, they always told the truth, unless someone else was with them, and then even if they were to be expelled for it they wouldn't give his name, even if he was a thief, which, as a matter of fact, he frequently was. It was surprising in such good schools, with fathers who never gave less than five quid, the number of thieves there were. The fellows in our school hardly ever stole, though they only got a penny a week, and sometimes not even that, as when their fathers were on the booze and their mothers had to go to the pawn.

I worked hard at the football and cricket, though of course we never had a proper football and the cricket we played was with a hurley stick against a wicket chalked on some wall. The officers in the barrack played proper cricket, and on summer evenings I used to go and watch them, like one of the souls in Purgatory watching the joys of Paradise.

Even so, I couldn't help being disgusted at the bad way things were run in our school. Our 'venerable pile' was a red-brick building without tower or pinnacle a fellow could climb, and no ghost at all: we had no team, so a fellow, no matter how hard he worked, could never play for the school and, instead of giving you 'lines', Latin or any other sort, Murderer Moloney either lifted you by the ears or bashed you with a cane. When he got tired of bashing you on the hands he bashed you on the legs.

But these were only superficial things. What was really wrong was ourselves. The fellows sucked up to the masters and told them all that went on. If they were caught out in anything they tried to put the blame on someone else, even if it meant telling lies. When they were caned they snivelled and said it wasn't fair; drew back their hands as if they were terrified, so that the cane caught only the tips of their fingers, and then screamed and stood on one leg, shaking out their fingers in the hope of getting it counted as one. Finally they roared that their wrist was broken and crawled back to their desks with their hands squeezed under their armpits, howling. I mean you couldn't help feeling ashamed, imagining what chaps from a decent school would think if they saw it.

My own way to school led me past the barrack gate. In those peaceful days sentries never minded you going past the guard-room to have a look at the chaps drilling in the barrack square; if you came at dinnertime they even called you in and gave you plumduff and tea. Naturally, with such temptations I was often late. The only excuse short of a letter from your mother, was to say you were at early Mass. The Murderer would never know whether you were or not, and if he did anything to you you could easily get him into trouble with the parish priest. Even as kids we knew who the real boss of the school was.

But after I started reading those confounded school stories I was never happy about saying I had been to Mass. It was a lie, and I knew that the chaps in the stories would have died sooner than tell it. They were all round me like invisible presences, and I hated to do anything which I felt they might disapprove of.

One morning I came in very late and rather frightened.

'What kept you till this hour, Delaney?' Murderer Moloney asked, looking at the clock.

I wanted to say I had been at Mass, but I couldn't. The invisible presences were all about me.

'I was delayed at the barrack, sir,' I replied in panic.

There was a faint titter from the class, and Moloney raised his brows in mild surprise. He was a big powerful man with fair hair and blue eyes and a manner that at times was deceptively mild.

'Oh, indeed,' he said, politely enough. 'And what delayed you?'

'I was watching the soldiers drilling, sir,' I said.

The class tittered again. This was a new line entirely for them.

'Oh,' Moloney said casually, 'I never knew you were such a military man. Hold out your hand!'

Compared with the laughter the slaps were nothing, and besides, I had the example of the invisible presences to sustain me. I did not flinch. I returned to my desk slowly and quietly without snivelling or squeezing my hands, and the Murderer looked after me, raising his brows again as though to indicate that this was a new line for him, too. But the others gaped and whispered as if I were some strange animal. At playtime they gathered about me, full of curiosity and excitement.

'Delaney, why did you say that about the barrack?'

'Because 'twas true,' I replied firmly. 'I wasn't going to tell him a lie.'

'What lie?'

'That I was at Mass.'

'Then couldn't you say you had to go on a message?'

'That would be a lie too.'

'Cripes, Delaney,' they said, 'you'd better mind yourself. The Murderer is in an awful wax. He'll massacre you.'

I knew that. I knew only too well that the Murderer's professional pride had been deeply wounded, and for the rest of the day I was on my best behaviour. But my best wasn't enough, for I underrated the Murderer's guile. Though he pretended to be reading, he was watching me the whole time.

'Delaney,' he said at last without raising his head from the book, 'was that you talking?'

''Twas, sir,' I replied in consternation.

The whole class laughed. They couldn't believe but that I was deliberately trailing my coat, and, of course, the laugh must have convinced him that I was. I suppose if people do tell you lies all day and every day, it soon becomes a sort of perquisite which you resent being deprived of.

'Oh,' he said, throwing down his book, 'we'll soon stop that.'

This time it was a tougher job, because he was really on his mettle. But so was I. I knew this was the testing-point for me, and if only I could keep my head I should provide a model for the whole class. When I had got through the ordeal without moving a muscle, and returned to my desk with my hands by my sides, the invisible presences gave me a great clap. But the visible ones were nearly as annoyed as the Murderer himself. After school half a dozen of them followed me down the school yard.

'Go on!' they shouted truculently. 'Shaping as usual!'

'I was not shaping.'

'You were shaping. You're always showing off. Trying to pretend he didn't hurt you—a blooming crybaby like you!'

'I wasn't trying to pretend,' I shouted, even then resisting the temptation to nurse my bruised hands. 'Only decent fellows don't cry over every little pain like kids.'

'Go on!' they bawled after me. 'You ould idiot!' And, as I went down the school lane, still trying to keep what the stories called 'a stiff upper lip,' and consoling myself with the thought that my torment was over until next morning, I heard their mocking voices after me.

'Loony Larry! Yah, Loony Larry!'

I realized that if I was to keep on terms with the invisible presences I should have to watch my step at school.

So I did, all through that year. But one day an awful thing happened. I was coming in from the yard, and in the porch outside our schoolroom I saw a fellow called Gorman taking something from a coat on the rack. I always described Gorman to myself as 'the black sheep of the school'. He was a fellow I disliked and feared; a handsome, sulky, spoiled, and sneering lout. I paid no attention to him because I had escaped for a few moments into my dream-world in which fathers never gave less than fivers and the honour of the school was always saved by some quiet, unassuming fellow like myself— 'a dark horse,' as the stories called him.

'Who are you looking at?' Gorman asked threateningly.

'I wasn't looking at anyone,' I replied, with an indignant start.

'I was only getting a pencil out of my coat,' he added, clenching his fists.

'Nobody said you weren't,' I replied, thinking that this was a very queer subject to start a row about.

'You'd better not, either,' he snarled. 'You can mind your own business.'

'You mind yours!' I retorted, purely for the purpose of saving face. 'I never spoke to you at all.'

And that, so far as I was concerned, was the end of it.

But after playtime the Murderer, looking exceptionally serious, stood before the class, balancing a pencil in both hands.

'Everyone who left the classroom this morning, stand out!' he called. Then he lowered his head and looked at us from under his brows. 'Mind now, I said everyone!'

I stood out with the others, including Gorman. We were all very puzzled.

'Did you take anything from a coat on the rack this morning?' the Murderer asked, laying a heavy, hairy paw on Gorman's shoulder and staring menacingly into his eyes.

'Me, sir?' Gorman exclaimed innocently. 'No, sir.'

'Did you see anyone else doing it?'

'No, sir.'

'You?' he asked another lad, but even before he reached me at all I realized why Gorman had told the lie and wondered frantically what I should do.

'You?' he asked me, and his big red face was close to mine, his blue eyes were only a few inches away, and the smell of his toilet soap was in my nostrils. My panic made me say the wrong thing as though I had planned it.

'I didn't take anything, sir,' I said in a low voice.

'Did you see someone else do it?' he asked, raising his brows and showing quite plainly that he had noticed my evasion. 'Have you a tongue in your head?' he shouted suddenly, and the whole class, electrified, stared at me. 'You?' he added curtly to the next boy as though he had lost interest in me.

'No, sir.'

'Back to your desks, the rest of you!' he ordered. 'Delaney, you stay here.'

He waited till everyone was seated again before going on.

'Turn out your pockets.'

I did, and a half-stifled giggle rose, which the Murderer quelled with a thunderous glance. Even for a small boy I had pockets that were museums in themselves: the purpose of half the things I brought to light I couldn't have explained myself. They were antiques, prehistoric and unlabelled. Among them was a school story borrowed the previous evening from a queer fellow who chewed paper as if it were gum. The Murderer reached out for it, and holding it at arm's length, shook it out with an expression of deepening disgust as he noticed the nibbled corners and margins.

'Oh,' he said disdainfully, 'so this is how you waste your time! What do you do with this rubbish—eat it?'

''Tisn't mine, sir,' I said against the laugh that sprang up. 'I borrowed it.'

'Is that what you did with the money?' he asked quickly, his fat head on one side.

'Money?' I repeated in confusion. 'What money?'

'The shilling that was stolen from Flanagan's overcoat this morning.' (Flanagan was a little hunchback whose people coddled him; no one else in the school would have possessed that much money.)

'I never took Flanagan's shilling,' I said, beginning to cry, 'and you have no right to say I did.'

'I have the right to say you're the most impudent and defiant puppy in the school,' he replied, his voice hoarse with rage, 'and I wouldn't put it past you. What else can anyone expect and you reading this dirty, rotten, filthy rubbish?' And he tore my school story in halves and flung them to the furthest corner of the classroom. 'Dirty, filthy, English rubbish! Now hold out your hand.'

This time the invisible presences deserted me. Hearing themselves described in these contemptuous terms, they fled. The Murderer went mad in the way people do whenever they're up against something they don't understand. Even the other fellows were shocked, and, heaven knows, they had little sympathy with me.

'You should put the police on him,' they advised me later in the playground. 'He lifted the cane over his shoulder. He could get the gaol for that.'

'But why didn't you say you didn't see anyone?' asked the eldest, a fellow called Spillane.

'Because I did,' I said, beginning to sob all over again at the memory of my wrongs. 'I saw Gorman.'

'Gorman?' Spillane echoed incredulously. 'Was it Gorman took Flanagan's money? And why didn't you say so?'

'Because it wouldn't be right,' I sobbed.

'Why wouldn't it be right?'

'Because Gorman should have told the truth himself,' I said. 'And if this was a proper school he'd be sent to Coventry.'

'He'd be sent where?'

'Coventry. No one would ever speak to him again.'

'But why would Gorman tell the truth if he took the money?'

Spillane asked as you'd speak to a baby. 'Jay, Delaney,' he added pityingly, 'you're getting madder and madder. Now, look at what you're after bringing on yourself!'

Suddenly Gorman came lumbering up, red and angry.

'Delaney,' he shouted threateningly, 'did you say I took Flanagan's money?'

Gorman, though I of course didn't realize it, was as much at sea as Moloney and the rest. Seeing me take all that punishment rather than give him away, he concluded that I must be more afraid of him than of Moloney, and that the proper thing to do was to make me more so. He couldn't have come at a time when I cared less for him. I didn't even bother to reply but lashed out with all my strength at his brutal face. This was the last thing he expected. He screamed, and his hand came away from his face, all blood. Then he threw off his satchel and came at me, but at the same moment a door opened behind us and a lame teacher called Murphy emerged. We all ran like mad and the fight was forgotten.

It didn't remain forgotten, though. Next morning after prayers the Murderer scowled at me.

'Delaney, were you fighting in the yard after school yesterday?'

For a second or two I didn't reply. I couldn't help feeling that it wasn't worth it. But before the invisible presences fled forever, I made another effort.

'I was, sir,' I said, and this time there wasn't even a titter. I was out of my mind. The whole class knew it and was awestricken.

'Who were you fighting?'

'I'd sooner not say, sir,' I replied, hysteria beginning to well up in me. It was all very well for the invisible presences, but they hadn't to deal with the Murderer.

'Who was he fighting with?' he asked lightly, resting his hands on the desk and studying the ceiling.

'Gorman, sir,' replied three or four voices—as easy as that!

'Did Gorman hit him first?'

'No, sir. He hit Gorman first.'

'Stand out,' he said, taking up the cane. 'Now,' he added, going up to Gorman, 'you take this and hit him. And make sure you hit him hard,' he went on, giving Gorman's arm an encouraging squeeze. 'He thinks he's a great fellow. You show him now what we think of him?'

Gorman came towards me with a broad grin. He thought it a great joke. The class thought it a great joke. They began to roar with laughter. Even the Murderer permitted himself a modest grin at his own cleverness.

'Hold out your hand,' he said to me.

I didn't. I began to feel trapped and a little crazy.

'Hold out your hand, I say,' he shouted, beginning to lose his temper.

'I will not,' I shouted back, losing all control of myself.

'You what?' he cried incredulously, dashing at me round the classroom with his hand raised as though to strike me. 'What's that you said, you dirty little thief?'

'I'm not a thief, I'm not a thief,' I screamed. 'And if he comes near me I'll kick the shins off him. You have no right to give him that cane, and you have no right to call me a thief either. If you do it again, I'll go down to the police and then we'll see who the thief is.'

'You refused to answer my questions,' he roared, and if I had been in my right mind I should have known he had suddenly taken fright; probably the word 'police' had frightened him.

'No,' I said through my sobs, 'and I won't answer them now either. I'm not a spy.'

'Oh,' he retorted with a sarcastic sniff, 'so that's what you call a spy, Mr Delaney?'

'Yes, and that's what they all are, all the fellows here—dirty spies!—but

I'm not going to be a spy for you. You can do your own spying.'

'That's enough now, that's enough!' he said, raising his fat hand almost beseechingly. 'There's no need to lose control of yourself, my dear young fellow, and there's no need whatever to screech like that. 'Tis most unmanly. Go back to your seat now and I'll talk to you another time.'

I obeyed, but I did no work. No one else did much either. The hysteria had spread to the class. I alternated between fits of exultation at my own successful defiance of the Murderer, and panic at the prospect of his revenge; and at each change of mood I put my face in my hands and sobbed again. The Murderer didn't even order me to stop. He didn't so much as look at me.

After that I was the hero of the school for the whole afternoon. Gorman tried to resume the fight, but Spillane ordered him away contemptuously — a fellow who had taken the master's cane to another had no status. But that wasn't the sort of hero I wanted to be. I preferred something less sensational.

Next morning I was in such a state of panic that I didn't know how I should face school at all. I dawdled, between two minds as to whether or not I should mitch. The silence of the school lane and yard awed me. I had made myself late as well.

'What kept you, Delaney?' the Murderer asked quietly.

I knew it was no good.

'I was at Mass, sir.'

'All right. Take your seat.'

He seemed a bit surprised. What I had not realized was the incidental advantage of our system over the English one. By this time half a dozen of his pets had brought the Murderer the true story of Flanagan's shilling, and if he didn't feel a monster he probably felt a fool.

But by that time I didn't care. In my school sack I had another story. Not a school story this time, though. School stories were a washout. 'Bang! Bang!'—that was the only way to deal with men like the Murderer. 'The only good teacher is a dead teacher.'

From *The Stories of Frank O'Connor*

For talking and writing

Frank O'Connor ran into trouble in this story because he behaved in an unexpected way. Murderer Moloney thought he was being impudent and defiant, and his classmates thought he had gone mad.

Have you ever been misunderstood because you behaved in a way that people didn't expect?

Frank says he wasn't paying much attention to Gorman in the classroom because he had escaped to his dream world for a few moments. His dream world was another kind of school with boys who behaved quite differently from the boys in his real school.

Write a story about a girl or a boy who keeps slipping away from real life into a dream world.

Who do you think were 'the invisible presences' that Frank keeps talking about? They seem to have been real enough to make him behave in a way that was mysterious to everyone in his real school. Do you think he felt himself surrounded by his companions from his dream world, or do you think they might have been his conscience in disguise?

Do you think your conscience is really part of you, or is it only your fear of the consequences?

Write a story called 'Conscience wins the Day' or 'Conscience loses . . . this time.'

Why do you think people get angry if you call them a liar? What is so important about telling the truth? Discuss some of the things which make it difficult.

Do you think children tell more lies than grown-ups?

Write down some of your thoughts on the subject.

What was it, in the end, that made Frank lose control of himself—defy the master, shout at everyone, threaten to go to the police, and then cry in his desk for the rest of the afternoon?

Write a story called 'Unfair'.

Most British schools have rules against fighting, though longer ago boys were allowed to settle their quarrels in *fair* fight i.e. one boy against another and no interference by friends or enemies. Red Indian boys on the other hand were trained from their earliest days to go on the Warpath and use any means to catch their enemies unawares (see section 9 Chief Plentycoups autobiography p. 152).

What are your views on the subject?

Do girls fight? If you don't fight with fists what can you use?

It has been said that stealing is an act of hostility. Do you agree or not? Is stealing by 5-year-olds different from stealing by 11-year-olds?

The boys in these school stories believed they shouldn't tell lies, shouldn't tell tales, and shouldn't make a fuss when they were whacked. Do you agree with this?

Do you think Frank had changed by the end of the story? Had he really given in? Was the change in the sort of books he read an act of surrender or a declaration of continued 'War'?

If you are interested in this story, carry on from where Frank left off.

Do you find this a serious or a funny story? or both?

Write a story called 'An odd sort of fight'.

Do you think it is anybody's job in a family to try to break up quarrels and keep the peace? Write your views on this.

Do you read the kind of school stories that have captured Frank's imagination? Discuss the stories you read.

4. Writing a Poem

Some of you will have written poems before; others may not know that all children can write poems, just as they can paint pictures or make things.

This section is about writing poems. It begins with some poems for you to read aloud and discuss.

Late

Late, O miller,

The birds are silent,

The darkness falls.

In the house the lights are lighted.
See in the valley they twinkle,
The lights of home.

Late, O miller,

The night is at hand,

Silence and darkness
Clothe the land.

R. L. STEVENSON

Try arranging this poem for three speakers and discuss how they should say it—loud—quiet—fast—slow—part of it in a whisper.

Some poems rhyme, and some don't. This one has only one rhyme. Why do you think it finishes with a rhyme?

But it has other kinds of patterns. Can you see what they are? The three speakers reading it aloud should help you to see these patterns.

These poems do not rhyme, but they all have some sort of pattern. Read them aloud, using two or three speakers, and then discuss which lines or parts of them you like particularly.

Later in the book you will find poems that rhyme, but if you try to use rhymes you will probably find that you have concentrated so hard on matching the rhyme pattern that you have forgotten what it was you really wanted to say, and all you have managed to produce is a jingle.

When you try reading 'Lullaby of a Woman of the mountains' aloud, you will see that it has a very simple pattern—two lines about the little grey mice; two lines about the insects; two lines about the birds that call in the night; and two final lines about all the night sounds.

A lullaby is a hushing song to send children to sleep feeling safe. You may like to write one addressed to the noises that you *hear when you are in bed and just falling asleep.*

'The Diver' and 'Night Clouds' have quite different patterns, and you will see what they are if you read them aloud.

Lullaby of a Woman of the Mountains

House, be still, and ye little grey mice,
Lie close tonight in your hidden lairs.

Moths on the window, fold your wings,
Little black chafers silence your humming.

Plover and curlew, fly not over my house,
Do not speak, wild barnacle, passing over the mountain.

Things of the mountain that wake in the night-time,
Do not stir tonight till the daylight whitens!

PADRAIC H. PEARSE

The Diver

I would like to dive
Down
Into this still pool
Where the rocks at the bottom are safely deep,

Into the green
Of the water seen from within,
A strange light
Streaming past my eyes—

Things hostile,
You cannot stay here, they seem to say;
The rocks, slime-covered, the undulating
Fronds of weeds—

And drift slowly
Among the cooler zones;
Then, upward turning,
Break from the green glimmer

Into the light,
White and ordinary of the day,
And the mild air,
With the breeze and the comfortable shore.

W. W. E. ROSS

Night Clouds

The white mares of the moon rush along the sky
Beating their golden hoofs upon the glass Heavens;
The white mares of the moon are all standing on their hind legs
Pawing at the green porcelain doors of the remote Heavens.
Fly, mares!
Strain your utmost,
Scatter the milky dust of stars,
Or the tiger sun will leap upon you and destroy you
With one lick of his vermilion tongue.

AMY LOWELL

Night Crow

When I saw that clumsy crow
Flap from a wasted tree,
A shape in the mind rose up:
Over the gulfs of dream
Flew a tremendous bird
Further and further away
Into a moonless black,
Deep in the brain, far back.

THEODORE ROETHKE

When I went to the Circus—

When I went to the circus that had pitched on the waste lot
It was full of uneasy people
Frightened of the bare earth and the temporary canvas
And the smell of horses and other beasts
Instead of merely the smell of man

The trapeze man, slim and beautiful like a fish in the air
Swung great curves through the upper space, and came down like a star
—And the people applauded with hollow, frightened applause.

The elephants, huge and grey, loomed their curved bulk through the dusk
And sat up, taking strange postures, showing the pink soles of their feet
And curling their precious live trunks like ammonites
And moving always with a soft slow precision
As when a great ship moves to anchor.

D. H. LAWRENCE

The next group of poems are all by school children. Read them aloud and discuss what you think of them.

The Departure

Goodbye, he called
Goodbye, I said
The puffs of smoke came out of the engine's funnel
And it slowly pulled out of the station.
I suddenly hated that big iron monster
For taking my friend away,
I felt that I could pull it apart
With my bare hands.

He called again
But as I called back
The sound of the engine drowned
My words.

PETER *aged* 13

The Quarry

The dull mist crept over the rock,
As I walked through the quarry.
Under my feet, dewy grass
Swished as I walked.
I looked over the quarry
Edge and I saw a cave and
Some hunting boys seeking
Fossils.
The ivy hangs like string from
The old man's garden.

RICHARD *aged* 12

Poem

After being committed for trial
A prisoner escaped from his cell.
His escape was discovered
The hunt began:
   In the woods I travelled
   In and out the trees;
   Strange noises I heard
   Like the animals at midnight
Then I was sitting under an apple tree:
I could hear the humming bee
Hopping from blossom to blossom
And see the birds that wipe their beaks
On the branches.

R. QUARRINGTON *aged* 14

The real test of a poem is to read it aloud: so do the same with the poems by young writers as you did with the first four poems in this section: arrange them in parts for two or perhaps three speakers and see how they sound after one or two rehearsals.

When some of you have written poems, read them aloud to see how they sound, preferably more than once. After discussing them, prepare a twenty-minute programme as for the radio, choosing some of the poems written in your class. There are several ways of arranging such a programme; for instance, you may choose poems on two or three special themes, such as 'Indoors and Out' or 'Night and Day' or 'Happy and Sad', etc., or you may just choose the ones you like best. You will need someone to make an introduction to the programme and explain what it is about: choose good readers.

5. Excursions and Returns

Before discussing what you think of the two stories about excursions by John and Stuart, write one of your own. Here are some suggestions:

How I spend my Saturdays: The circus; Visiting relations; Guy Fawkes night; Listening to grown-ups; A visit to the dentist; Homecoming; Setting off on a journey; A visit to Grandpa's; Going to hospital; Interesting things I have found on the beach; Moving house; The picnic; Staying out late; Being lost; Out in the fog; Night journey.

A visit to the Zoo

On my return from school on Wednesday afternoon my father invited me to accompany him on a visit to the Zoological Gardens. I answered in the affirmative and we at once boarded a tramcar bound for the city. Here we caught the omnibus, and soon arrived at our destination.

We had heard such a lot of talk about the new polar bear pit, that we decided to visit this modern structure first of all. After a good discussion on this piece of workmanship, we made our way to the Monkey Temple. Here we had a gay half-hour watching the peculiar antics of the monkeys, who seemed almost human in some respects. We then partook of a frugal tea, and continued our tour by a visit to the noisy parrot house. . . . On looking at the clock we saw that it was twenty minutes past seven, so we concluded our journey by viewing the humming birds.

We soon arived back to our abode, and I retired to bed, feeling that I had gleaned much knowledge during the evening.

What do you think of John's attempt to describe his visit to the Zoo? There is a lot to be said both for and against it. What sort of thing has he left out? Look closely at the words and expressions he uses and consider what effect they have on you.
Now read 'The Dog with a Million Fleas' and see what you think of that. There is a lot to say about it. Apart from its greater length, what can you notice about it?

The Dog with a Million Fleas

I heard my mother calling me and groaned, time to get up again. The edges of my window panes sparkled with frost and the sky looked grey, as though it were going to snow. And then I remembered, it was Saturday, the best day of the whole week. I lay there warm and snug and planned what I would do. I know! I would go to the copse. As long as I can remember my sister and I have made up special names for people, places and things. 'The Grand Canyon' for instance is a dale we often visit for picnics and 'Little Egypt' is a hillock with some trees on top, and 'The Copse' is a name which we gave to the grounds surrounding an old house which has since been pulled down. It is a magic sort of place where one can always find something unusual, there my sister and I have spent many a happy hour wandering about and imagining all sorts of things there. We have often seen a family of hedgehogs, and are careful not to frighten them as they are rather timid at first. It is a favourite haunt of birds, and there is an old square well, but we pretend it is a wishing well, and we have found two beehives tucked away among the undergrowth, empty now but once they were used. The house was standing then and people lived in it and I expect they were very happy at least my sister and I like to think so, and so I decided to go to the copse again, and I wondered what I would discover today. The best things always happen to me on a Saturday except Christmas and birthdays as they happen on any day of the week.

I dressed and had my breakfast, mummy made me put on two pairs of socks and then my wellingtons and she said it was going to snow. I put my scarf and gloves on too and pretended I was an explorer in the arctic wastes. I slipped my penknife into my pocket and two russets from the box in the pantry. In the autumn when our apples are ready for picking, we gather them and wrap them up in paper, then in winter we have a good supply to munch at, they have a nice taste and the skins are very wrinkled, at night mummy puts a bowl on the hearth and we all help ourselves.

Now my penknife is a very special one, and I have never seen another like it, and I feel very proud when people ask to see it, for it has two blades, a corkscrew, a saw, a tin opener, screwdriver, an awl and even a pair of scissors. My uncle gave it to me for my birthday four years ago, it was not new when he gave it to me, for he had it during the war, and he knew that I admired it more than anything else in the world, and although I have had lots of nice presents for Christmas and birthdays this one seemed my best.

So I felt very happy as I went down the lane with the penknife and apples in my pocket. I wished I had brought my dog Dandy with me as he loves exploring too, he is not an ordinary dog, everyone else seems to have dogs like poodles, dachshunds and dogs like that, but my dog is a cross-bred terrier, some people say he's only a mongrel, and I tell them that he's cleverer than any dog I've ever met, he can play hide and seek and he doesn't cheat either! You can leave him in the potting shed, and tell him to stay and hide his eyes, then hide yourself and whistle him, and he always finds you, he joins in all our games and he is four years old, and we bought him for twelve and six from the Manchester Dogs Home and mummy says he's the best twelve and six-pennyworth she has ever seen. Anyway I must tell you about my visit to the copse when I got there the ground was white with frost and it made everything look different. I didn't see any birds or anything at all, the copse seemed quiet and deserted but a little dog with a rough curly coat came trotting up to me, it barked at first but when I talked to it a little it wagged its tail and let me pat it, every so often it shook itself sat down and started to scratch furiously and then I heard a whistle and looked up and saw a boy, he was about 9 years old and had a nice friendly sort of face and he smiled at me. 'That's my dog', he said, 'He's called Ruff'. I told him I had a dog too. All the time we were talking I was looking at him. He looked very cold as his clothes seemed too small for him, his jacket sleeves were very short and his thin wrists stuck out, and his hands were very red, he kept rubbing them together. He was a thin sort of boy and very cheerful and I liked him a lot. He said he had never been to the copse before. I showed him my penknife while we were talking and I could see he thought it was marvellous. He kept on opening and shutting the blades and cutting little bits of wood that lay about. And then he said rather sadly, 'I wish I had one like it', and I said, 'Why don't you ask your father to buy you one for Christmas?' He said very quickly, 'I haven't got a father'. I could tell by the way he spoke he didn't want to say any more, so I offered him an apple. He bit a piece off for his dog and then asked me what made the skins wrinkled like that. 'It's a russet', I said. 'My father picks them from the trees and puts them by for winter'. 'Have you got your own apple trees', he said in surprise, 'How many have you got'. I was just going to say eight when I stopped. How could I say I had eight apple trees when he hadn't even got a father. 'Oh we've only got one', I said, 'And it's not a very good one either'. 'This tastes all right to me', he said. All the time he had been talking to me, his little dog had been running round and jumping up at him and licking his hands, you could see the dog loved him. And he would bend down and rub the dog's ears and fuss him as if he loved him too, and every so often the dog would shake himself violently and scratch himself first one place and then another, it made me tickle all over just to look at him. 'Why does he keep shaking and scratching', I asked. 'Oh!' he said, 'He can't help it, he's got flees'. 'Fleas?' I said. 'Yes', he said proudly, 'He's got about a million of them'. 'Doesn't he mind', I said. 'Oh no', he answered. 'He's always had them'. What with scratching and shaking and jumping and licking he was the funniest little dog I have ever seen.

The boy took something from his pocket. 'Look at this', he said. It was a large marble and it had a lovely coloured whirly line going round inside it. He told me to look through it, and I did so, it looked beautiful and he was very pleased when I told him it was the best one I had ever seen. 'Would you like it', he said. 'Oh no I couldn't take it', I told him. 'Go on', he said, 'I want you to have it'. He pressed it in my hand and said, 'I must go now. I'll come again next week'. He whistled his dog who was scratching as though his life depended on it, he bounded after the boy, and off they went, when he came to the trees he turned and waved, and I waved back, I still had the marble in one hand and my penknife in the other, in a moment the boy and dog had gone.

I stood there feeling very miserable I had such a lot of things, I could easily have given him the knife. He only had a marble and he had given that to me.

I went home and went up to my room to think it over, my dog came with me, I sat on my bed and he pushed his nose into my hands, he knew how I felt, he may not have fleas but he's very understanding. I put the marble and penknife in my top drawer and went downstairs. I told mummy all about it and asked her what I should have done and she asked me what I would do if the same thing should happen all over again and I said that I would give him the knife, so I made up my mind that if he came the next week I would give it him. Now in nearly all books I have read the stories have had happy endings but this one hasn't. Although I went back to the copse many times I didn't see the boy or dog again. It doesn't seem the same magic place any more, the workmen have been and cut down most of the trees and it's just a large space now.

Mummy said when I asked her why, 'Nothing ever stands still things are changing all the time'.

It all happened a long time ago, but I still have the penknife and marble. I don't suppose I will ever see him again, it used to make me feel unhappy but when I think of the boy now I don't feel sad about him any more. My mother said that anyone with a nice little dog like Ruff couldn't help feeling happy. So I think of him as I last saw him waving to me through the trees with his little dog jumping up and down and running round him, the dog that loved him best in the world, the dog with a million fleas!

STUART *aged* 12

This story was read and discussed with a class of 11-year-old girls as a preliminary to their own writing. It caused much discussion. They thought the boy would one day be a great writer; however, he seemed a little childish for his age.

Were they right? Do people go on playing imaginary games till they are quite old? Some people thought it might be memories of something that happened when he was younger. This could be found out by looking carefully at the text. Others thought it might have been entirely made up. It was agreed that it didn't matter whether it was made up, or remembered, or a bit of each.

They said they enjoyed discussing writing by people of about their own age, as they felt free to judge according to their *own* standards of merit.

Boredom and Enjoyment

One day, on my Easter Holiday at Liverpool, mum and dad decided to go and look at the site where we were thinking of moving. It was at Fleetwood a few miles from Liverpool. They also decided to take a look at the kind of homes which were to be built.

We waited impatiently for mum to prepare lunch excited that we were soon to see what might be our future house. When all was ready the seven of us, three grown-ups, two teenagers (my sisters) and one girl of eleven and myself went in the car. My sister and I sat in the small luggage compartment at the back of our Morris Traveller and it was very uncomfortable in the confined space.

On the way we ate nearly all the sandwiches. The traffic was so heavy that it was a long time till we reached Fleetwood. On the way my parents and my auntie talked about things which they had done and things which had happened to them. I tried to join in the conversation but they didn't seem to be interested with what I had to say and it was hard to get a word in edgeways without interrupting.

It was so uncomfortable that I tried to move from the spot I had been sitting for the past fifteen minutes. But this seemed to irritate or hurt my sister Sandra so she hit me then I hit her back. This developed into a fight but we were soon controlled by our mother. This made us unfriendly to each other and therefore unfriendly with my other sister and my cousin.

After a while I began to get bored because there was nothing to do. It was raining outside and we were crawling along because there was a hold-up. I felt very depressed because there was so much I could do back in Liverpool and so much I wanted to do. I kept on wanting to go to sleep because I felt all achy and I kept on getting pins and needles. I wanted to sleep it off. But I couldn't because it was so uncomfortable and I can never seem to get to sleep when it is light although it was a dull and miserable day which added to my discomfort.

I began thinking about something to do but there was nothing not even a pencil and paper and Sandra still disliked me.

KENNETH *aged* 12

Write about a time when you were miserable and uncomfortable.

'The Summer of the Beautiful White Horse' was written by an Armenian whose family had emigrated to California.

There is certainly an excursion in this story and a different kind of return.

The Summer of the Beautiful White Horse

One day back there in the good old days when I was nine and the world was full of every imaginable kind of magnificence, and life was still a delightful and mysterious dream, my cousin Mourad, who was considered crazy by everybody who knew him except me, came to my house at four in the morning and woke me up by tapping on the window of my room.

Aram, he said.

I jumped out of bed and looked out of the window.

I couldn't believe what I saw.

It wasn't morning yet, but it was summer and with daybreak not many minutes around the corner of the world it was light enough for me to know I wasn't dreaming.

My cousin Mourad was sitting on a beautiful white horse.

I stuck my head out of the window and rubbed my eyes.

Yes, he said in Armenian. It's a horse. You're not dreaming. Make it quick if you want a ride.

I knew my cousin Mourad enjoyed being alive more than anybody else who had ever fallen into the world by mistake, but this was more than even I could believe.

In the first place, my earliest memories had been memories of horses and my first longings had been longings to ride.

This was the wonderful part.

In the second place, we were poor.

This was the part that wouldn't permit me to believe what I saw.

We were poor. We had no money. Our whole tribe was poverty-stricken. Every branch of the Garoghlanian family was living in the most amazing and comical poverty in the world. Nobody could understand where we ever got money enough to keep us with food in our bellies, not even the old men of the family. Most important of all, though, we were famous for our honesty. We had been famous for our honesty for something like eleven centuries, even when we had been the wealthiest family in what we liked to think was the world. We were proud first, honest next, and after that we believed in right and wrong. None of us would take advantage of anybody in the world, let alone steal.

Consequently, even though I could *see* the horse, so magnificent; even though I could *smell* it, so lovely; even though I could *hear* it breathing, so exciting; I couldn't *believe* the horse had anything to do with my cousin Mourad or with me or with any of the other members of our family, asleep or awake, because I *knew* my cousin Mourad couldn't have *bought* the horse, and if he couldn't have bought it he must have *stolen* it, and I refused to believe he had stolen it.

No member of the Garoghlanian family could be a thief.

I stared first at my cousin and then at the horse. There was a pious stillness and humour in each of them which on the one hand delighted me and on the other frightened me.

Mourad, I said, where did you steal this horse?

Leap out of the window, he said, if you want to ride.

It was true, then. He *had* stolen the horse. There was no question about it. He had come to invite me to ride or not, as I chose.

Well, it seemed to me stealing a horse for a ride was not the same thing as stealing something else, such as money. For all I knew, maybe it wasn't stealing at all. If you were crazy about horses the way my cousin Mourad and I were, it wasn't stealing. It wouldn't become stealing until we offered to sell the horse, which of course I knew we would never do.

Let me put on some clothes, I said.

All right, he said, but hurry.

I leaped into my clothes.

I jumped down to the yard from the window and leaped up on to the horse behind my cousin Mourad.

That year we lived at the edge of town, on Walnut Avenue. Behind our house was the country; vineyards, orchards, irrigation ditches, and country roads. In less than three minutes we were on Olive Avenue, and then the horse began to trot. The air was new and lovely to breathe. The feel of the horse running was wonderful. My cousin Mourad who was considered one of the craziest members of our family began to sing. I mean, he began to roar.

Every family has a crazy streak in it somewhere, and my cousin Mourad was considered the natural descendant of the crazy streak in our tribe. Before him was our uncle Khosrove, an enormous man with a powerful head of black hair and the largest moustache in the San Joaquin Valley, a man so furious in temper, so irritable, so impatient, that he stopped anyone from talking by roaring, *It is no harm: pay no attention to it.*

That was all, no matter what anybody happened to be talking about. Once it was his own son Arak running eight blocks to the barber shop where his father was having his moustache trimmed to tell him their house was on fire. This man Khosrove sat up in the chair and roared, It is no harm; pay no attention to it. The barber said, But the boy says your house is on fire. So Khosrove roared, Enough, it is no harm, I say.

My cousin Mourad was considered the natural descendant of this man although Mourad's father was Zorab, who was practical and nothing else. That's how it was in our tribe. A man could be the father of his son's flesh, but that did not mean that he was also the father of his spirit. The distribution of the various kinds of spirit of our tribe had been from the beginning capricious and vagrant.

We rode and my cousin Mourad sang. For all anybody knew we were still in the old country where, at least according to some of our neighbours, we belonged. We let the horse run as long as it felt like running.

At last my cousin Mourad said, Get down. I want to ride alone.

Will you let me ride alone? I said.

That is up to the horse, my cousin said. Get down.

The *horse* will let me ride, I said.

We shall see, he said. Don't forget that I have a way with a horse.

Well, I said, any way you have with a horse, I have also.

For the sake of your safety, he said, let us hope so. Get down.

All right, I said, but remember you've got to let me try to ride alone.

I got down and my cousin Mourad kicked his heels into the horse and shouted, *Vazire*, run. The horse stood on its hind legs, snorted, and burst into a fury of speed that was the loveliest thing I had ever seen. My cousin Mourad raced the horse across a field of dry grass to an irrigation ditch, crossed the ditch on the horse, and five minutes later returned, dripping wet.

The sun was coming up.

Now it's my turn to ride, I said.

My cousin Mourad got off the horse.

Ride, he said.

I leaped to the back of the horse and for a moment knew the awfulest fear imaginable. The horse did not move.

Kick into his muscles, my cousin Mourad said. What are you waiting for? We've got to take him back before everybody in the world is up and about.

I kicked into the muscles of the horse. Once again it reared and snorted. Then it began to run. I didn't know what to do. Instead of running across the field to the irrigation ditch the horse ran down the road to the vineyard of Dikran Halabian where it began to leap over the vines. The horse leaped over seven vines before I fell. Then it continued running.

My cousin Mourad came running down the road.

I'm not worried about you, he shouted. We've got to get that horse. You go this way and I'll go this way. If you come upon him, be kindly, I'll be near.

I continued down the road and my cousin Mourad went across the field towards the irrigation ditch.

It took him half an hour to find the horse and bring him back.

All right, he said, jump on. The whole world is awake now.

What will we do? I said.

Well, he said, we'll either take him back or hide him until tomorrow morning.

He didn't sound worried and I knew he'd hide him and not take him back. Not for a while, at any rate.

Where will we hide him? I said.

I know a place, he said.

How long ago did you steal this horse? I said.

It suddenly dawned on me that he had been taking these early morning rides for some time and had come for me this morning only because he knew how much I longed to ride.

Who said anything about stealing a horse? he said.

Anyhow, I said, how long ago did you begin riding every morning?

Not until this morning, he said.

Are you telling the truth? I said.

Of course not, he said, but if we are found out, that's what you're to say. I don't want both of us to be liars. All you know is that we started riding this morning.

All right, I said.

He walked the horse quietly to the barn of a deserted vineyard which at one time had been the pride of a farmer named Fetvajian. There were some oats and dry alfalfa in the barn.

We began walking home.

It wasn't easy, he said, to get the horse to behave so nicely. At first it wanted to run wild, but, as I've told you, I have a way with a horse. I can get it to want to do anything *I* want it to do. Horses understand me.

How do you do it? I said.

I have an understanding with a horse, he said.

Yes, but what sort of an understanding? I said.

A simple and honest one, he said.

Well, I said, I wish I knew how to reach an understanding like that with a horse.

You're still a small boy, he said. When you get to be thirteen you'll know how to do it.

I went home and ate a hearty breakfast.

That afternoon my uncle Khosrove came to our house for coffee and cigarettes. He sat in the parlour, sipping and smoking and remembering the old country. Then another visitor arrived, a farmer named John Byro, an Assyrian who, out of loneliness, had learned to speak Armenian. My mother brought the lonely visitor coffee and tobacco and he rolled a cigarette and sipped and smoked, and then at last, sighing sadly, he said, My white horse which was stolen last month is still gone. I cannot understand it.

My uncle Khosrove became very irritated and shouted, It's no harm. What is the loss of a horse? Haven't we all lost the homeland? What is this crying over a horse?

That may be all right for you, a city dweller, to say, John Byro said, but what of my surrey?[1] What good is a surrey without a horse?

[1] Surrey: a light cart.

Pay no attention to it, my uncle Khosrove roared.

I walked ten miles to get here, John Byro said.

You have legs, my uncle Khosrove shouted.

My left leg pains me, the farmer said.

Pay no attention to it, my uncle Khosrove roared.

That horse cost me sixty dollars, the farmer said.

I spit on money, my uncle Khosrove said.

He got up and stalked out of the house, slamming the screen door.

My mother explained.

He has a gentle heart, she said. It is simply that he is homesick and such a large man.

The farmer went away and I ran over to my cousin Mourad's house.

He was sitting under a peach-tree, trying to repair the hurt wing of a young robin which could not fly. He was talking to the bird.

What is it? he said.

The farmer, John Byro, I said. He visited our house. He wants his horse. You've had it a month. I want you to promise not to take it back until I learn to ride.

It will take you a *year* to learn to ride, my cousin Mourad said.

We could keep the horse a year, I said.

My cousin Mourad leaped to his feet.

What? he roared. Are you inviting a member of the Garoghlanian family to steal? The horse must go back to its true owner.

When? I said.

In six months at the latest, he said.

He threw the bird into the air. The bird tried hard, almost fell twice, but at last flew away, high and straight.

Early every morning for two weeks my cousin Mourad and I took the horse out of the barn of the deserted vineyard where we were hiding it and rode it, and every morning the horse, when it was my turn to ride alone, leaped over grape vines and small trees and threw me and ran away. Nevertheless, I hoped in time to learn to ride the way my cousin Mourad rode.

One morning on the way to Fetvajian's deserted vineyard we ran into the farmer John Byro, who was on his way to town.

Let me do the talking, my cousin Mourad said. I have a way with farmers.

Good morning, John Byro, my cousin Mourad said to the farmer.

The farmer studied the horse eagerly.

Good morning, sons of my friends, he said. What is the name of your horse?

My Heart, my cousin Mourad said in Armenian.

A lovely name, John Byro said, for a lovely horse. I could swear it is the horse that was stolen from me many weeks ago. May I look into its mouth?

Of course, Mourad said.

The farmer looked into the mouth of the horse.

Tooth for tooth, he said. I would swear it *is* my horse if I didn't know your parents. The fame of your family for honesty is well known to me. Yet the horse is the twin of my horse. A suspicious man would believe his eyes instead of his heart. Good day, my young friends.

Good day, John Byro, my cousin Mourad said.

Early the following morning we took the horse to John Byro's vineyard and put it in the barn. The dogs followed us around without making a sound.

The dogs, I whispered to my cousin Mourad. I thought they would bark.

They would at somebody else, he said. I have a way with dogs.

My cousin Mourad put his arms around the horse, pressed his nose into the horse's nose, patted it, and then we went away.

That afternoon John Byro came to our house in his surrey and showed my mother the horse that had been stolen and returned.

I do not know what to think, he said. The horse is stronger than ever. Better-tempered too. I thank God.

My uncle Khosrove, who was in the parlour, became irritated and shouted, Quiet, man, quiet. Your horse has been returned. Pay no attention to it.

From *My Name is Aram* by WILLIAM SAROYAN

For discussion

Aram says about the Armenian people 'We were proud first, honest next, and after that we believed in right and wrong.'

Aram had a difficult time with his conscience. Do you agree with his various arguments to himself?

Do you think the boys had stolen the horse, or borrowed it? What makes the difference between stealing and borrowing?

Do you think there is a difference between reasons and excuses?

How must the incident have looked to the farmer, John Byro? He never accuses the boys of having stolen his white horse. What do you think of the way he got the boys to return it?

Why do you think Mourad says the horse is called 'My Heart'.

Discuss anything that strikes you as unusual about this story.

Every family has a crazy streak in it somewhere. Has your family? Who is the 'craziest' person you know?

Discuss which of the stories in this section you like best.

For writing

Write a story in which you borrow something; describe how you returned it.

Write about the person in your family you are most like. (Think about your grandparents, your cousins, and your aunts and uncles as well as your parents and brothers and sisters.)

Write a story containing the words 'I couldn't believe my eyes'.

Write a story called 'The Three Wishes'. Try to make this a long, full story with interesting people and some conversation in it. If you could have some extraordinary power such as being invisible, or weightless, or being able to turn yourself into something else, which would you choose? You might write about this and describe one of the occasions when you used this power.

Mongolian boys on horseback

OTHER WORLDS

6. Animals and Suchlike

G

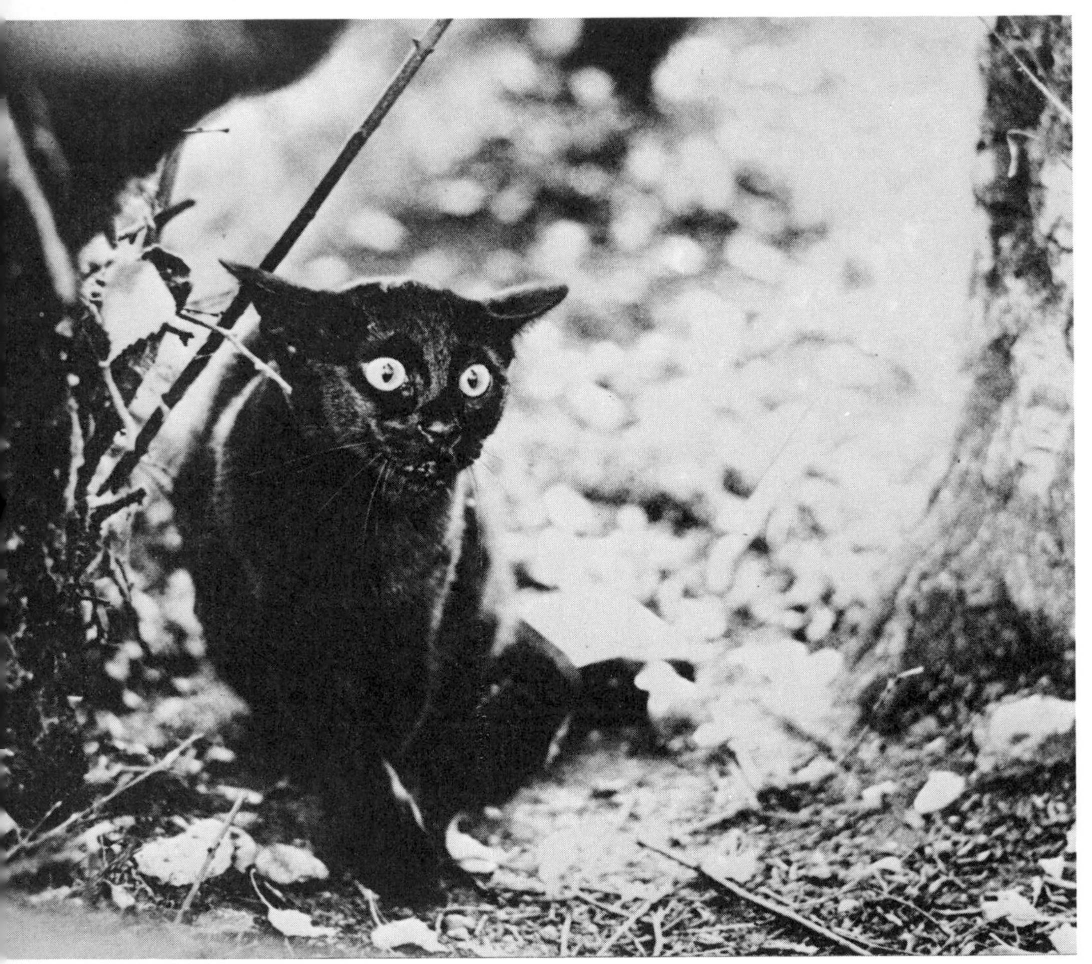

Here are two passages by Konrad Lorenz, a scientist who studies animal behaviour. Not only has he a very sharp eye for observing all sorts of things about his pets, but it is clear that he is very fond of them and finds them very amusing.

Cat!

The threatening attitudes of a cat are extraordinarily expressive, and are entirely different in their manifestation according to whom they are directed against: whether they apply to a human friend who has 'gone too far', or to a feared enemy, perhaps a dog or another cat. They are different, too, according to whether they are made purely in self-defence or whether they imply self-assurance in the animal and predict a forthcoming attack. Cats always announce their intention of attacking, and, . . . they never bite or scratch without giving previous unmistakable warning to the offender. Usually, indeed, the gradually increasing threatening gestures are suddenly exaggerated just before action is taken; this is evidently an ultimatum, 'If you don't leave me alone at once, I shall unfortunately be obliged to take reprisals'.

The cat threatens dogs—or any other dangerous preying animals—by making its well-known 'hunch back'. Standing on straight, stiff legs and making itself as tall as possible, it ruffles the hair of back and tail, holding the latter slightly to one side in order to make its whole dimensions appear larger to the enemy, almost as some fishes do in self-display or to intimidate a foe. The cat's ears are laid flat, the corners of its mouth are pulled backwards, the nose is wrinkled. From its chest a low, strangely metallic growl issues, which culminates now and again in the wellknown 'spitting', that is, a forced expiration during which the throat is wide open and the incisors exposed. In itself, this threatening gesture is doubtless meant to be defensive; it is most frequently seen when a cat suddenly finds itself face to face with a big dog and has no time to withdraw. Should the dog come nearer in spite of this warning, the cat does not flee but attacks as soon as the dog has overstepped a certain, definite 'critical distance'. It hurls itself at the dog's face and, with claws and teeth, savages its most sensitive places, if possible the eyes and nose. Should the dog show the least sign of flinching, the cat regularly makes use of this slight breathing space to take flight. Thus the short feline attack is only to gain time while finding a way of escape.

Man meets Dog by KONRAD Z. LORENZ

Jackdaw!

Another tame adult male jackdaw fell in love with me and treated me exactly as a female of his own kind. By the hour, this bird tried to make me creep into the nesting cavity of his choice, a few inches in width, and in just the same way a tame male house sparrow tried to entice me into my own waistcoat pocket. The male jackdaw became most importunate in that he continually wanted to feed me with what he considered the choicest delicacies. Remarkably enough, he recognised the human mouth in an anatomically correct way as the orifice of ingestion and he was overjoyed if I opened my lips to him, uttering at the same time an adequate begging note. This must be considered as an act of self-sacrifice on my part, since even I cannot pretend to like the taste of finely minced worm, generously mixed with jackdaw saliva. You will understand that I found it difficult to co-operate with the bird in this manner every few minutes! But if I did not, I had to guard my ears against him, otherwise, before I knew what was happening, the passage of one of these organs would be filled right up to the drum with warm worm pulp—for jackdaws, when feeding their female or their young, push the food mass, with the aid of their tongue, deep down into the partner's pharynx. However, this bird only made use of my ears when I refused him my mouth, on which the first attempt was always made.

King Solomon's Ring, by KONRAD Z. LORENZ

Have you noticed particular things about the behaviour of your pets, or do you think of them as human beings in disguise? Clearly the jackdaw regarded Konrad Lorenz as a bird in disguise!

Write your own piece about some animal whose behaviour and habits you have observed carefully.

Some things you might find out by watching carefully are:

How a cat gets the milk into its mouth by lapping.
How a dog fetches a stick or ball (does he watch you or the stick?).
How can you tell whether dogs are fighting or merely playing?
How do cows go through a gate? Do they queue up or go in any particular order?
How does a bird land on a branch or perch?

A collection of pieces of writing about different animals might be put together to make a book that is as interesting, and true, as Lorenz's books.

The two following passages are by schoolgirls. They are about themselves as well as about the animals they describe.

Discuss what is in them. (Feelings, information, imagined feelings, questioning.)

The True Story of a Little Sparrow

One lunch hour 18 months ago my daddy came home from work with a small box and put it in the kitchen, I peeped inside it and there was a tiny little sparrow about 1 inch long he was only a few hours old, he must have fallen from his nest into a truck at the warehouse where my daddy works. He was hardly moving. Mommy said, 'What have you brought that here for?' (because only the day before Mommy had had quite a shock and was frightened when a starling came down the chimney and flew out when she was clearing the fire.)

The sparrow was an ugly little thing and almost dead, but we padded a chocolate box with cotton-wool and wrapped him in it and brought him in the warm by the fire. We put a little bread on the end of a matchstick and tried to feed him by putting it inside his mouth. We tried for a long time and eventually he swallowed some. We laid the box on a hot water bottle to keep him warm, which we kept changing as it went cooler. We kept him alive all day by feeding him a little at a time. Next morning we did not expect him to be alive but he gradually began squeaking and opening his mouth for food; we looked after him and in a few days his little pink body began to go a grey colour and little slits began to appear for his eyes, and his mouth became an orange colour and his squeaking became much stronger. After about five days his little eyes opened and he began to notice things around him. We decided to give him a name and called him 'Boy'. Boy continued to get stronger still living in the little chocolate box and squeaking for food. A few more weeks went by and he began to go fluffy and feathers began to appear, then he did not look so ugly and mommy began to like him and could pick him up. He liked to keep his nest clean. He would climb out of his nest, jump on the floor and try to fly across the floor to daddy when he called him. We had to be very careful not to tread on him so we decided to put him in the cage with our budgie during the daytime. He sat on the perch squeaking away and nightime we put him back in his nest. Whitsuntide came round and we went to Nan's for the holiday, of course Boy had to come with us, on the bus in my little basket. I bet there are not any more little sparrows who if they could talk could say they had been for a ride on a bus, a car, and even on his first journey here in a saddle-bag on daddy's cycle. Now today Boy is as lively and as happy as can be, he feeds himself off his little dish to bread and milk and helps himself to the budgie's seed. He often comes out of the cage and sits on my shoulder waiting for food. He loves cake, jelly, pears, potato, carrot and the funniest thing to see is him eating ice-cream off a spoon. The budgie and Boy are great friends and play on the floor together and at Christmas it was nice to see them both flying to the Christmas tree. Little Boy is happy to be living with us; I wonder if he realized what a lucky little sparrow he is, and although we call him Boy we find we really should have called her 'Girl' but we could not change his name now.

ANGELA

Sonnet to a Bear born in the Zoo

Little white bear-cub, snowy-sleek and round,
Forget the gaping crowds and the orange peel they throw,
Forget the stagnant pond and the twopenny buns you found,
And dream of the land that your mother used to know,
Where the sparkling ice glitters green and sapphire blue
In the shimmering curtain of the fiery Northern lights,
Where swim the shiny seals that your parents caught and slew,
When the snow lay deep in the frozen winter nights.

Follow your mother to the greasy, lukewarm pool,
And listen to the snow and ice that cracks beneath her feet,
For you're dreaming of the north, where the racing wind is cruel,
And you can't hear the children and the traffic in the street.
So forget your clumsy clownishness and dream that you are free,
A swift fierce hunter in the icy Arctic sea.

CELIA *aged* 12

Here are some subjects to start you thinking and talking and writing about animals (or birds).

Looking through binoculars.
A day in the life of a wild animal.
Training a puppy.
My animal friends.
Pets I have known.
The pet shop.
The chimpanzee that escaped from the zoo.
Finding a bird's nest.
Swans.
The white blackbird.
The mouse's tale.
The insect.
Watching a snake.

You may want to describe something very exact such as the location and construction of a swan's nest that you examined; or the order in which you do things in training a puppy; or you may want to write a poem as Celia did, about a polar bear that she saw at the zoo; or you may write a fantastic or amusing story about a chimpanzee (or any other animal) that escaped from the zoo; or an imaginary story about a day in the life of a wild animal.

Ted Hughes tells us how a fox jumped into his mind one night; and how he 'caught' it and kept it 'alive'.

An animal I never succeeded in keeping alive is the fox. I was always frustrated: twice by a farmer, who killed the cubs I had caught before I could get to them, and once by a poultry keeper who freed my cub while his dog waited. Years after those events I was sitting up late one snowy night in dreary lodgings in London. I had written nothing for a year or so but that night I got the idea I might write something and I wrote in a few minutes the following poem: the first animal poem I ever wrote. Here it is.

The Thought Fox

I imagine this midnight moment's forest:
Something else is alive
Beside the clock's lonliness
And this blank page where my fingers move.

Through the window I see no star:
Something more near
Though deeper within darkness
Is entering the lonliness:

Cold, delicately as the dark snow,
A fox's nose touches twig, leaf;
Two eyes serve a moment, that now
And again now, and now, and now

Sets neat prints into the snow
Between trees, and warily a lame
Shadow lags by stump and in hollow
Of a body that is bold to come

Across clearings, an eye,
A widening deepening greenness,
Brilliantly, concentratedly,
Coming about its own business

Till, with a sudden sharp hot stink of fox
It enters the dark hole of the head
The window is starless still; the clock ticks,
The page is printed.

TED HUGHES

This poem doesn't have anything you could easily call a meaning. It's about a fox, obviously enough, but a fox that is both a fox and not a fox. What sort of fox is it that can step right into my head where presumably it still sits . . . smiling to itself when the dogs bark. It is both a fox and a spirit. It is a real fox; as I read the poem I see it move, I see it setting its prints, I see its shadow slipping over the irregular surface of the snow. The words show me all this, bringing it nearer and nearer. It is very real to me. The words have made a body for it and given it somewhere to walk. If I hadn't caught the real fox there in the words I would never have saved the poem. I would have thrown it into the wastepaper basket. As it is, every time I read the poem the fox comes up again out of the darkness and steps into my head. And I suppose that long after I'm gone, as long as a copy of the poem exists, every time anyone reads it the fox will get up somewhere out in the darkness and come walking towards them.

Was this a real fox?

Is it alive?

Here is what Susie wrote about a fox.

Fox

My father saw a fox last night
And nobody believed him.

Upstairs we heard him open the backdoor
It was a windy night last night
The moon was out.

My father said he saw the fox sitting
                quite still
                in the yard.
'What did it look like?' we said
                unbelieving.
'Smaller than a dog,' he said
                smiling.

The fox's eyes had glinted in the
                light from the kitchen.
It started, turned, and disappeared
Into the shadows on the lawn.

My father saw a fox last night
And nobody believed him.

For writing

Thoughts jump in and out of our minds as the fox did in Ted Hughes's poem. If we catch them before they jump out again, and put them down on paper, we have got them, possibly for ever. Then we possess something like the thought fox that was both real and imaginary, or like Susie's fox that nobody believed in. When you write your next piece see if you can really capture it in words. You may know immediately what you are going to write about; if you don't you may like to try writing on 'Something I shall never forget'.

Read your own story through and see if it really has got on to paper what you saw and felt and thought.

Make a programme for reading aloud from five or six of the pieces that people have written. Practice reading them before you give the performance.

If there are enough that you like, they might be made into a book.

Here are two pieces about a bird and a fox.

What do you think of them?

What do you think the writers have captured in these stories?

The Blackbird

In our garden there is a large blackbird who comes down every day. I feed him worms and bread. Mostly I feed him worms because I like the way he breaks them up. First he flies down from the roof on to the fence. Then he makes out he can't see me but he is watching me all the time. If I make a sudden move he will take to the air. He approaches the worm with the skill of a gladiator. He cuts the worm into about eight pieces with sword-like blows from his beak. He always makes sure that no other birds eat his worms. If they try to, he will pick it up and bring it nearer to me, because he is not afraid of me but the other birds are. Four pieces of the worm are eaten, and the other pieces are taken to his nest.

JOHN

Fox!

Christene and I went for a walk across the fields to pick daffodils for the chalets. The sheep stared at us while the lambs ran to their mothers. We crossed the stream and made our way towards a field which we knew never failed to be filled with daffodils. Half way across the field Christene stopped and asked me what I thought a brown lump was that was lying in the field a little further on. After a few seconds we agreed on it being a fox. We rushed down the hill towards it and at once saw that it was a vixen and it had been shot in the legs. She was a horrid sight, her front legs were clotted with blood and her mouth was bleeding. She had died angry with her teeth in a snarling position. Her eyes were bloodshot and had sunk in.

I was angry that anybody had dared to kill her. My stomach bubbled up with rage and I sobbed. Her ears were velvety and black and soft, her tail was like a large clump of soft red feathers. Oh . . . she was so beautiful.

Christene must have been as angry as I, for she kept saying that if they killed foxes for eating chicken they should kill us, and I quite agreed with her. For the second time I stroked her soft ears and then it occured to us that she might have cubs somewhere, so we set about to dig her a grave and then we would look for her cubs.

We tried to dig up the turf with my pen-knife, but it was slow going. So we decided to take her down to the stream where there was some soft mud. Neither of us wanted to carry her, so we took turns and I am sorry to say that by the time we got her down to the stream she had more than a few bumps. With our hands we dug a small pit and laid her in. We then covered her up with mud and put four crosses on top, which were made of different things such as twigs, grass and waterweed. After doing this we said a short prayer for foxes and then we trudged off over the fields. We were too unhappy to have the heart to look for her cubs, so instead we went to the farm to see the cats, but for the rest of the day we couldn't stop thinking how cruel some farmers and men were.

ANNA

Alsatian

As I am coming home from school a big
Alsatian greets me,
His light green eyes begin to stare at me,
For I know he hates me, and I
Certainly hate him.
He begins to show his teeth, and begins to
Snarl at me.
I tell it to shoo but it takes no notice,
I stamp my foot, then suddenly it starts
To bark,
The baby next door starts to cry,
Then to my relief the owner whistles
And it starts to run on by.

JOHN *aged* 11

Do you feel this way about any dogs?

7. Ghosts and Mysteries

Here is a story told by a French girl called Catherine Legrand. The 'You' in the story is Catherine herself speaking.

The Ghost in the Forest

You went into the forest this afternoon. You found periwinkles and jonquils. You made them into posies which you stuck in your belt so you could keep on running more easily. You ate lunch in a clearing. You sat in a circle. Mademoiselle leaned against the trunk of a beech tree. You drew straws to see who would tell a story. You cut pieces of wood into sticks which were all the same length except one. Mademoiselle held them in her hand in a bunch so all the ends were even. You took turns picking sticks. Anne Marie Losserand drew the one that was shorter than the others. She told the story of a princess who is mistreated by her stepmother and stepsisters. These women are wicked and ugly. The princess is beautiful and good. The princess is not allowed to go to the ball. But she puts a chicken wing on her head, an onion peel around her neck she puts on the cook's apron and waits in her room for the fairy to come and fix everything with her wand and make the chicken feather beautiful and iron the apron.

Anne Marie Losserand's story is very long. Mademoiselle smiles and nods her head as she listens. The undergrowth gets darker. Mademoiselle tells Anne Marie Losserand that she may finish her story tomorrow in class that they must leave right away or they will not be home before dark. You get up. You throw away the posies you have in your belt, the stems are broken and the flowers with their drooping heads are useless. Catherine Legrand leaves the silk scarf which her mother lent her on condition that she did not lose it at the foot of the beech tree.

You are in the playground. It is already completely dark except for a dim glow where the sun went down. Catherine Legrand suddenly remembers that she left the scarf under the beech tree. She wants to go back right now. She says she won't get lost that she knows the way very

Carved heads from a mountain Temple in Cambodia

well. Mademoiselle doesn't want Catherine Legrand to go alone into the forest at night. Catherine Legrand says I will take Reine Dieu, we know the way. Reine Dieu says Yes yes let's go. Mademoiselle says I forbid you. Mademoiselle says that there is a ghost in the forest, that it is very foolish to go there now because he is there at night and that if Reine Dieu and Catherine Legrand go there they will die. No one knows what a ghost is. She says it is a dead person who leaves his grave that you can tell he is a ghost because he has his shroud over his head, that he waits for people and sucks blood from their throats. You laugh. But you aren't very sure that Mademoiselle is joking. You ask her if it is true. She says it is. She says she would never go into Saints' Forest at night because of the ghost. You ask her how she knows this. She says that a gentleman she knows has seen it. But then the ghost didn't suck his blood? No, he managed to escape because he was a man and because he didn't lose his self-control. And what does the ghost do when there is nobody in the forest? He waits for someone to come. And what if nobody goes there? He keeps on waiting. Probably he has plenty of time. Reine Dieu says in Catherine Legrand's ear, We're going anyway.

You don't dare talk too loud on the road. You say goodbye without mentioning the forest again. Reine Dieu has turned left to go towards the church. Catherine Legrand keeps on straight ahead until she comes to the national highway where she turns right. Ahead on the road the reflector moves like the lamps divers hold in their hands in stories. What if it weren't a reflector at all? What if it were the red lamp of the altar in the hand of a dead person? Of course you don't have to believe in that ghost business; but even so Mademoiselle really tells it that way, as if it were true, as if she were really afraid of them. Catherine Legrand stops in the road. There isn't any other way to get home. You have to go straight ahead it's the only thing to do you have to brave it since behind you all the doors of the school are closed there isn't anybody left in the playground or in the classroom now. Catherine Legrand starts to run to get it over with sooner. The road is all dark. You manage to cheer yourself up with the thought of the two street lamps which you come to as soon as you turn off the road on to the national highway. In just a few moments you'll be there, in the zone of light.

Mother says What's all this about a ghost? She knits her brow as she does when Catherine Legrand tells a lie, You must have misunderstood, there are no such things as ghosts, that's what you heard, you can't possibly have heard the opposite, think about it a little and you'll see that ghosts do not exist. Fine, that's what Mother says. But Mademoiselle nodded her head and rolled her eyes up and down and to the sides meaning Yes it is true there are ghosts in the forest. So in the end you have no idea what ghosts are and whether they exist or not.

From *The Opoponax* by MONIQUE WITTIG

For discussion or writing

Do you think ghosts exist?

Draw lots as the French children did for a story-telling session and tell a story you know and like.

Write on one of these:

Going home in the dark.

A bad dream or nightmare.

Things you were afraid of when you were much younger.

An alarming person.

A kindly ghost.

The haunting motorbike.

A frightening animal.

A story so blood-curdling that it makes the readers laugh.

A frightening tale you have been told and half believe or used to believe.

A short programme of mysterious and ghostly stories.

The Griesly Wife

'Lie still, my newly married wife,
Lie easy as you can.
You're young and ill accustomed yet
To sleeping with a man.'

The snow lay thick, the moon was full
And shone across the floor.
The young wife went with never a word
Barefooted to the door.

He up and followed sure and fast,
The moon shone clear and white.
But before his coat was on his back
His wife was out of sight.

He trod the trail wherever it turned
By many a mound and scree,[1]
And still the barefoot track led on
And an angry man was he.

He followed fast, he followed slow,
And still he called her name,
But only the dingoes[2] of the hills
Yowled back at him again.

His hair stood up along his neck,
His angry mind was gone,
For the track of the two bare feet gave out
And a four-foot track went on.

[1] A scree is a stony slope. [2] Dingoes are wild Australian dogs.

Her nightgown lay upon the snow
   As it might upon the sheet,
But the track that led on from where it lay
   Was never of human feet.

His heart turned over in his chest,
   He looked from side to side,
And he thought more of his gumwood fire
   Than he did of his griesly bride.

And first he started walking back
   And then began to run
And his quarry wheeled at the end of her track
   And hunted him in turn.

Oh, long the fire may burn for him
   And open stand the door,
And long the bed may wait empty:
   He'll not be back any more.

JOHN MANIFOLD

Dicky

Mother: Oh, what a heavy sigh!
Dicky, are you ailing?

Dicky: Even by the fireside, Mother,
My heart is failing.

Tonight across the down,
Whistling and jolly,
I sauntered out from town
With my stick of holly.

Bounteous and cool from sea
The wind was blowing,
Cloud shadows under the moon
Coming and going.

I sang old country songs,
Ran and leaped quick,
And turned home by St Swithin's
Twirling my stick.

And there, as I was passing
The churchyard gate,
An old man stopped me: 'Dicky,
You're walking late.'

I did not know the man,
I grew afeared
At his lean, lolling jaw,
His spreading beard.

His garments old and musty,
   Of antique cut,
His body very frail and bony,
   His eyes tight shut.

Oh, even to tell it now
   My courage ebbs . . .
His face was clay, Mother,
   His beard, cobwebs.

In that long horrid pause
   'Good night,' he said,
Entered and clicked the gate:
   'Each to his bed.'

Mother: Do not sigh or fear, Dicky;
   How is it right
   To grudge the dead their ghostly dark
   And wan moonlight?

We have the glorious sun,
   Lamp and fireside.
Grudge not the dead their moonbeams
   When abroad they ride.

ROBERT GRAVES

Lammerlinkin

Lam - mer-lin - kin was as good a mas-on as e'er built with
stone He— built a fine— cas - tle but— pay - ment got none.

'Oh pay me Lord Wearie—or I swear and I vow
That before you come home you will have cause to rue'.

Says Lord Wearie to his lady, as he mounted his horse,
'Beware of Lammerlinkin who lives on the moss.'

'Let the doors all be bolted and the windows all pinned,
Don't leave a window open for Lammerlinkin.'

He kissed the fair lady and he then rode away,
For he must be in London by the dawning of the day.

'Where's the lord of his house?' says Lammerlinkin.
'He's gone to fair London,' says the false nurse to him.

'Where's the heir to this house?' says Lammerlinkin.
'In his cradle a-sleeping,' says the false nurse to him.

'Then we'll pinch him and we'll prick him and make him to cry,
And the lady will come down for to see the reason why.'

So they pinched him and they pricked him all over with a pin,
And the false nurse held the bowl for the blood to run in.

'Oh but nurse how you slumber, Oh nurse how you sleep;
You leave my little baby to cry and to weep.'

'But I've tried him with milk and I've tried him with the pap;
Come down my fair lady and rock him in your lap.'

'Oh how can I come down so late in the night,
When there's no fire a burning and no candle-light?'

'You have three silver lanthorns that shine in the sun;
Come down my fair lady by the light of one of them.'

Then the lady came down, she was thinking no harm,
Lammerlinkin was waiting and caught her by the arm.

There was blood in the kitchen, there was blood in the hall,
There was blood in the parlour where the lady did fall.

The servant being up in the window so high,
She saw her master coming and she began to cry;

'Oh don't blame me, Lord Wearie, don't blame me,' said she,
'It was the false nurse and Lammerlinkin that killed your lady.'

Lammerlinkin he was hung in the gibbet so high,
And the false nurse she was burned in the fire just nearby.

Things to do with this group of stories

The Griesly Wife

Let someone re-tell the story of the griesly wife as fully and vividly and hauntingly as possible.

Read it aloud, as for a performance, perhaps with three speakers, a 'husband' who speaks the first verse, and two 'narrators'; the second narrator to begin reading where the man's anger is suddenly changed to fear.

Dicky

Read this poem with two speakers, Dicky and his Mother. Try to find some music to introduce this poem and to play when it is finished. The mood of the first music might echo Dicky's alarm and horror at his encounter with the ghost. The mood of the concluding music should reflect his Mother's kindliness even to a poor ghost.

Lammerlinkin

This is an old story; both the others were modern ones. Let one person tell it in his own words as dramatically as he can manage.

Try out an acted version and a mimed version with no words.

If you can, learn the tune, and get a small group to sing it; or if anyone is willing, a single singer.

Discuss which best conveys the horror of the things that happened:

The sung version.

The ballad read by a single speaker.

Acted with a narrator and characters.

Mimed.

The re-telling in prose.

Perform it again in one of these ways.

Discuss which would be the best order for these three ballads in a performance and why.

Give the performance.

If you want to lengthen the performance, hunt through books of poems, ballads and stories for one or two more items; or write some yourselves.

For writing

Write any story about a haunting or a murder that you want to write. It may be one you have heard or read, or you may prefer to invent it.

Write the story of the griesly wife as if it were told by the husband—but it will, of course, have to end where 'his quarry wheeled at the end of her track'.

Write a letter to a gentle ghost; describe what you did with the letter and whether anything happened.

Here is another kind of mystery.

On the top of a Surrey hill above a steep valley stands a stone called The Gibbet Stone. On it is inscribed

ERECTED

In detestation of a barbarous deed
committed here on an unknown sailor
On Sept. 24th 1786
By Edwd Lonegon, Mich. Casey and Ja^s^ Marshall
who were all taken on the same day
and hung in chains near this place.

'Whoso sheddeth man's blood
By man shall his blood be shed'.

Genesis. Chap 9. Verse 6.

Discuss what in fact, did happen as far as we know—and what might have been the happenings that led to this stone being erected.

Write a story either of your own invention or on one of the subjects over the page. Or you may prefer to write a play.

The Unknown Sailor

Ask yourself these sort of questions before you write.

Who was the unknown sailor?

What was he doing on the Surrey hill-top?

How was it no-one knew anything about him?

The Three Irishmen

Ask yourself; What were the murderers like? What were they doing in England? How did they meet the sailor? Did they know him or come upon him by chance? Was the murder the result of a chance quarrel or was it planned? How do you think they were 'taken'? Was there an uproar? a witness? Was there a chase and a capture? Did one of them inform against the others?

Write the story of what happened as you imagine it.

Eye-witness

Imagine there was a witness of this horrid deed.

Write the story he would have told many times in his life to his friends, to his children, and to his grandchildren. Try to write it as if he were telling it as an old man (or woman) to his (or her) grandchildren. He would remember the scene very vividly—the lonely road, the trees, the heathery banks, the night—what he saw and heard, and felt, and what he did.

'The Price of a Bride' is an old story retold by Ted Hughes.

The Price of a Bride

Huntsman I am the king's huntsman.
I see the hidden fawn reflected
In the eye of the eagle
That hangs under the cloud.

When the howling of wolves
Wakes me after midnight
I hear the wind altered
And the stag turned on the mountain.
By the boar's hoofprint in snow
I get my apple barrels ready.
I do not worry much
About the King's worries.
But now I see two.
Through the heavy forest
Where the trees are normal,
Where the stones are of plain stone
And where the water
Is reliably water,
And where the shadows
Are in quiet agreement
With the old sun,
Through our ancient land
Two horsemen are riding,
Riding to find a bride,
Riding to fight a ghost,
Riding to fight the ghost
That guards the King's daughter.
This is good news.
None can defeat this ghost.
And the horse dies under the warrior.
And my hounds get horsemeat.
They are always ready for horsemeat.

Enter the brothers, Tor and Tormil

Tor I'd see my sword a poker,
My helmet a coal-scuttle,
My armour patching kettles
And be killed by a wood-cat

And eaten by her kittens
Before marry some daft woman
And be killed by prattle.

Tormil You've the brawn of a man, brother,
But the words of a boy.

Tor What is a knight's job?
Hacking cruel heads off,
Splitting wicked hearts,
Slashing solid rashers
Off enormous ogres,
Abridging the miles of monster,
Work of the noble weapon.
Not simpering at home,
Your brain rotten with perfume.

Tormil Brother, do you think
You dropped off a bush in the wood?
Our father understood:
Wives must be had,
Be they good or bad.
So I'm riding to win this bride
And you'll be my spokesman.

Tor What about this ghost.

Tormil Ghosts do not exist.
Steel exists. And blood.
Bones and death exist.
Ghosts do not exist.

Tor Every suitor before you
Has agreed about it.
All have had to meet it.

A great grey grisly warrior
On the ghost of a great horse.
He was so real they lost.
And most ghostly of all:
Each one lost a finger
From inside his gauntlet,
A gauntlet full of blood.

Tormil Ghost do not exist.

Tor It charged and it struck
In a blue flash—bam!
A blue glare, like lightning.
And their horses died on the spot.

Tormil Ghost do not exist.
Ghosts eat nobody.
Ghosts do not exist.

Huntsman The bluetit in the birchtree
Watches the brothers go by.
The weasel under the root
Pauses and smells their horses
Then bolts from their laughter.
The buzzard in the rainbow
Sees their red cloaks floating.
And comes circling lower.
Their eyes enjoy primroses.
Their dappled stallions step.
The smoky catkins tremble.
Ah, they are still young.
And the great mistakes
Are still only blossoms.
It is still possible
That they will be lucky,

That their luck will come
While they have their strength
In this leafy land.
Though the bones in the earth,
The bones the blades have scarred,
The disappointed bones,
That the dog has cracked,
Are waiting for the worst
Under the blind soil.

TED HUGHES

From *A stag hunt at night* by PAOLO UCCELLO

For discussion (possibly in pairs)

What was the price of this bride?

What did Tor think a Knight's job was?

What does Tormil believe in?

In what ways are the brothers different?

Do either of the brothers really want the bride?

What kind of a man does the King's huntsman seem to be?

What creatures, people, things are watching—and waiting?

What do you think they are waiting for?

For speaking and writing

This story was written for radio, so only the speakers' voices carry the story.

Choose three people with very different voices to read the parts.

Rehearse it several times.

If you can use a tape-recorder, put it on tape and discuss whether the readers have managed to make it sound foreboding and ghostly.

You might use this as a further item in the programme of mysteries and terrible stories. You might include music and sound effects.

Some suggestions for stories and poems.

The Wolves.

Lost in the Forest.

The Watcher in the Woods.

'My hounds are always ready for horsemeat.'

The King's Huntsman remembers.

Shadows in the Moonlight.

'There were no lights in any windows and the tall streets of the city were completely silent . . . .'

Take one or two lines of the story and write about them in any way you like. Make them the start of your own story—or the start of a poem.

8. Today and Yesterday

Uncle William's Christmas presents. Drawing by JOHN GILBERT, 1856

Yesterday

Here are two stories written *for children* about 150 years ago. They are very different from the stories written for children today. In Appendix 8 you will find more about children's books in the past.

The Spoiled Children

Mr. Beaufoy had two sons whom he tenderly loved, but did not spoil. He gave them an excellent education, and inured them to such habits as promised to render their constitutions healthy and vigorous. Though he possessed a handsome fortune, he seldom permitted them to partake of rich meats or to drink wine; he also accustomed them to early rising, to washing themselves with cold water, to sleeping in a cold bed in the winter, and to taking daily exercise without fearing a little wind or rain.

Mr. Robinson's children were very differently managed; they had coffee, chocolate, wine, tarts, and all sorts of sweetmeats, as often as they thought proper; water was warmed in the morning to wash them; their beds were warmed in the evening; and they were not permitted to go out if the weather were cold or cloudy.

One day, Philip and James were talking with their father; and, without presuming to complain of the manner in which they were educated, they happened to say, according to what they had heard, that the little Robinsons were very happy.

Mr. Beaufoy, to undeceive them, proposed to them to go with him to pay a visit to Mr. Robinson, whose home was at the distance of some miles from his own. This proposition was received with joy; and the next morning, they set out in a post-chaise.

The journey was a very cheerful one; but when they arrived, what a sight presented itself to their eyes!

On entering the apartment, they saw three children in the most miserable condition: their faces yellow, their eyes dull and hollow, their teeth black and broken; and they were altogether so weak and so meagre, that people might have supposed they did not get enough to eat.

Mrs. Robinson complained with tears in her eyes, that for eight days past, her fourth son had been obliged to keep his bed; and, soon after, she brought a large glass of medicine, and made each of the children drink his share.

At table, Mr. Robinson's children appeared to be disgusted with every thing, and to care for nothing. On the other hand, their guests, Philip and James, ate cheerfully of whatever was set before them. There was even a plate of cucumbers, a vegetable rather indigestible, of which they ate heartily.

Mrs. Robinson asked them, with an air of concern, if so doing would not make them ill? and she added, that she should think her children would be killed if she permitted them to taste such food.

She was perfectly astonished when they replied, that they were used to such things, and that nothing made them ill.

Some time after they had dined, Mr. Beaufoy took leave of Mr. and Mrs. Robinson; and on returning home, he sent his children to their cold bed at an early hour as usual.

The next day, they came skipping to wish their papa good morning: their little cheeks were as red as roses, and an air of health gave lustre to their whole countenance.

'How happy I am,' said their papa, 'to have children so gay, and so healthy! I should be truly afflicted if I saw you languid and weak like the Robinsons. What do you think of those children?'

'O dear, papa,' replied Philip, 'those poor children excite our pity: they look like shadows; and appear as if they were going to die. We would not be in their place for all the gold in the world.'

'But,' replied their father, 'if I were to rear you as tenderly as they are reared; if I had your bed warmed, and the water, in which you are to wash, heated; if I were to give you wine and chocolate; if, instead of the simple meats which we have at dinner, I should teach you to relish some dainty, would you not be better pleased?'

'No, no, papa!' cried they, 'we prefer cold beds and cold water, and nothing but plain food, to being made sick with rich meats and warm beds.

'I am delighted, my dear boys,' said the father, 'that you know how to prize the health you enjoy. I hope that you will never again envy the lot of the little Robinsons, and that you will understand that your father, in educating you with less delicacy, only seeks your happiness.'

The lesson which Mr. Beaufoy gave to James and Philip was but too forcibly illustrated by what happened afterward to Mr. Robinson's children. The boy that was ill when Mr. Beaufoy visited that gentleman, died in the course of a few days. Two other sons, also, died in the following year, and in this manner:—Seeing, one day in the winter, some children at play upon the ice, they had a great desire to take part in the amusement: they went, therefore, to their mother, and persuaded her to walk for half an hour with them. On returning to the house, however, it appeared that they had taken a violent cold; and though their mother put them to bed, and made them take various medicines, they died in a few days.

Only the eldest son now remained; and though he did not die so early as the others, he was the subject of illness all his life.

At the age of twenty-four, he was as weak as an old man, and was obliged to have a fire in his chamber every day; for even in summer, he complained that he was never warm. His stomach was so weak that it could bear nothing but boiled veal, lamb, or chickens; and he one day expected to die because he had eaten a small slice of bacon. So true it is, that those who wish to enjoy good health, should be accustomed to a hardy mode of life.

From *Idle Hours Employed*, a collection of moral tales by JOHN HARRIS (1826)

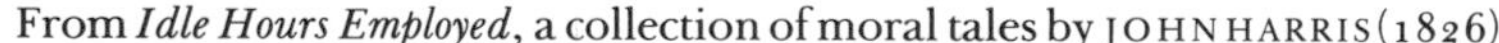

Filial Affection

Volney Beckner, who was born at Londonderry in Ireland, felt an early desire for the sea—perhaps from his father being by profession a sailor.

He had only reached his twelfth year, when he served with his father in an English vessel. His father, who knew by experience the dangers which a mariner runs, had taught him to swim; so that he cut the waves, plunged, and swam on the surface of the water with nearly as much facility and lightness as a fish! His greatest amusement, when his other occupations would permit him, was to swim round the vessel, and when he was weary, he would seize a cord, and in an instant leap on board the ship.

One day the child of a passenger, a very little girl, by means of the rolling of the ship, fell into the sea. The father of Volney, who happened to be present, sprang in after her, and soon caught her by the clothes; but as this brave mariner was regaining the vessel, and holding the child close to his bosom, he perceived a terrible shark pursuing him.—The shark is a large and strong fish, with an enormous mouth, armed with teeth, which cut and break the hardest bone.—The whole crew ran to the part where Beckner was trembling for his life, and fired their carbines at the monster, yet none durst go to his assistance.—The shark, who was not wounded, had already opened his horrid mouth, and was about to seize his prey, when a hideous shriek was given by all on board.

At the same moment, some one was observed to leap into the water. It was young Volney, armed with a large pointed sabre. He immediately plunged in, and went straight to the shark, which, stopping for a moment, gave him time to slide under his belly, into which he struck the sabre to the very hilt, and the desire of saving his father gave additional force to his arm; but Volney avoided him, and gave him several fresh stabs.—During this combat they had thrown from the ship's side several ropes, and the father and the son each seized one.—They were drawn out of the sea, and every one began to rejoice.—Their comrades thought them safe; but, horrid to relate! at that moment the monster, furious with his wounds, and still more furious at losing his prey, made a last and powerful effort. He plunged deep in the water, in order to take a more vigorous spring, and then, throwing himself above the waves, raised his horrid open mouth, and swallowed half the body of the young Volney, separating it from the other half, which remained suspended by the cord. This direful spectacle petrified all the spectators, and old Beckner, arrived on board, was in the utmost despair at having survived his son; but the son cast his last look upon the author of his life and seemed, even while dying, to feel pleasure in having preserved his father from the fatal accident of which he himself became the victim.

From *The Parental Instructor; or, A father's present to his children* (1820)

For discussion

What do you think of these stories?

Do you like either of them?

Are they like anything else you have read?

Are the children in these stories like any children you know?

How are the stories that you read different from these?

Since grown-ups write most of the stories that children read, something must have changed since the early 1800s. What do you think has changed? Children's taste in stories, or adults' views of what children like, or adults' views of what children ought *to like?*

Today

Here are two stories by school children.

The Tyre

Fairly recently a park has been made from an old rubbish tip quite near to where I live. This park is bordered by a stream, and on the other side of the stream is a large area which is completely overgrown with trees and shrubs, and is, quite naturally a paradise for the children of the neighbourhood. In one part of it is 'the tyre'. This is, as the name suggests, a heavy motor tyre, probably from a large lorry, fixed to a limb, high up in one of the tallest trees, by a length of thick steel cord. How this was ever secured up there is a mystery to many of those who have been there, as their tree seems virtually unscaleable, but there it was and was a focal point for many of the older boys who used to congregate there. I used to be quite satisfied just swinging backwards and forwards on it or maybe swinging off from a low branch. A friend of mine, as were several others, was more adventurous. He would climb a tree which was just about within the arc formed by the tyre and would get someone to swing up the tyre to him. Grabbing hold of the tyre, he would let go of the tree and go soaring down to the ground, only to be swung high up into the air again on the other side. Watching this looked simple and good fun, but for a long time I never tried it.

Then one day my friend suggested that I should have a go at it. At the time there was another boy there who had also done it several times and who probably thought nothing of it, so I was determined to have a try. I struggled up the tree which was, by the way, a difficult tree to climb anyway. Quite near the top was a narrow limb, on which, I was told, one was meant to balance, higher up from the ground than a double-decker bus. I was already quaking so much that I feared I would shake myself off the branch. Then came the difficult bit. I had to cling onto the tree and then lean out as far as I possibly could in order to reach the heavy tyre as it came flying towards me. After a few wasted efforts it was carefully explained to me that I was not far out enough on the branch and so moving fractionally out I at last managed to grab hold of the tyre.

Just then I decided that I could not do it and shouted out my intentions to those below, who had now grown in number from two to four. A deep sigh came from those below and seemed to signify that they were all getting fed up. If I went down now, I realised, I would not be able to face them again for quite a while after so I decided to do it.

It was not as easy as it may sound though. The tyre, being at its maximum distance, was tending to pull me off the branch, so, in the split second in which I would let go of the tree, I would have to quickly get a secure hold of the tyre with both hands. I slowly counted one . . . two . . . three . . . and then took a deep breath, but no, I still could not face it.

After what seemed like an eternity to me and must have seemed even longer to those below who were now starting to pass comments, I took another deep breath and . . . let go of the tree. All that fuss—just for that. It was quite a pleasant experience soaring down through the air and I was up like a shot for another go, quite ready to make fun of any newcomers who had difficulty in their first try!

IAN

A Memory

Since my mother had parted from my father we had lived with my nanny and grandad. They lived in a pleasant house in good surroundings. My mother we saw only in the evenings, the rest of the day she worked to provide for me and my older brother. My grandad couldn't work anymore owing to a disease, silicosis.

Sometimes in the morning we would watch my mother go to work. Through the fence we could see her as she walked down the lane, waving till she rounded the corner and disappeared. We used to jump down the steps by the gate and run down the steep path back to the house for another lonely day. About five minutes to nine my brother was taken down to the Infants School. I used to stand by the gate crying as he marched down the road.

Down at the bottom of the garden was a pigsty and an old seat whereupon my grandad used to sit with me upon his knees. I would sit and look up at the face of my grandfather and ask him why he had a moustache. He would tell me a different story each time about the wars and when he lived on a farm. While he was engrossed in his story I would play with his nailless forefinger. I can always remember this finger, I would sit for hours just poking it and biting it clasped in my hands. My grandad would sit and laugh and pat Bessie on her hind-quarters whereupon she would squeal and take shelter in the pigsty so I looked down the food channel at the large pig making noises as she ate her food. Sometimes grandfather would lift me high in the air and sit me on the wall.

My grandfather used to cough rather badly and I just stared and looked up at the red face covered by a large red and white spotted hanky shaking up and down. At times I was very frightened by these coughing spells which began to come more frequently as summer came to a close.

Many times my grandad used to take me for a ride on his bike; a cushion was tied securely on the cross bar and I used to sit there looking down at the road and the front wheel spinning. Often we went to some fields near our home where I would take off my shoes and my grandfather stooped low to roll up my dungarees so that I could paddle in the clear beck. My grandfather used to sit resting and breathing deeply although we were only a short distance from home. When it was time to go home I would pick daisies and buttercups in handfuls along with the grass and chase the yellow and coloured butterflies all round the field. These happy times were soon to finish I didn't understand about death only the withering of the flowers and leaves on the trees. I still wasn't old enough for school when on a warm day my mother didn't go to work and grandad stayed in bed. I asked why and was told grandad was ill and may leave us. I wanted to know if I could go with him and why could't I. I was carried up the stairs and I ran into my grandad's bedroom. I climbed onto the chair then onto the bed and over the ocean of blankets up to my grandad. He put his arm round me and kissed me and then he started to cry. I was frightened and cried too; when my mother took me off the bed I screamed to go back. I pushed past my mother biting her hand and saw my nanny by the bed saying prayers, quietly crying over the blankets covering my grandad. I never knew what happened and I was shocked by the loneliness; many times I sat in the black-currant bushes with a bedraggled teddy bear crying for my grandad. I used to go into the hut and stare at the bike. This is one memory I will always cherish of someone who was good and kind.

DIANNE

For discussion and writing

Which of these do you like best?

Which do you admire most? (These may not be the same.)

Which of these manage to get a real person down on paper as well as tell a story?

In what ways are these real stories by young writers different from the stories written for children in the first part of this section?

Which do you prefer—the stories written by *children or the stories written* for *children.*

A class of boys who read these stories racked their brains to think what things were like 150 years ago—scurvy, no toothpaste, sailors who couldn't swim, they said. They came to the conclusion that these kinds of stories weren't necessary nowadays, because there are other ways of teaching the lessons they contained: there are red flags on the beaches when sharks are about, posters for dental care, and swimming lessons for school children, etc.

What are your views?

The boys also said that they liked horror stories but that these two were unsuitable for young children because of the deaths.

What do you think?

Write about an occasion when you were surprised by the way another family behaved.

Write a story about a 'bad child'.

9. Lost World

A totem, two inches high. A coyote squats on a man's head.

Myths are stories about human beings and gods—about the natural and the supernatural. Many of them are 'explanations' of things that were important but puzzling to people of ancient times, such as the coming and going of the sun in summer and winter, the stars, the winds, floods and earthquakes.

The first story in this section is a myth told by the North American Indians of the Cheyenne tribe who roamed the great prairies and followed the buffaloes on whom they depended for food and clothing. When the prairies were ploughed and broken up into farms by the white settlers the roaming life of the Indians and of the buffalo both came to an end.

How the Seven Brothers Saved Their Sister

Long and long ago, there lived among the Cheyennes an old woman and her young granddaughter. They had no other relatives, and lived together in a little lodge, where the grandmother taught the young girl, Red Leaf, to make fine beaded robes and moccasins. Nowhere in all the tribe was there a better robe-maker than Red Leaf.

Now it so happened that not very far from there lived seven brothers. They had no father, no mother, and no sisters. The seven of them lived together, with the youngest, Moksois, staying at home to take care of the camp while the six older brothers went out to hunt.

'Grandmother,' said Red Leaf, one day, 'I would like to have Moksois and his brothers to be my brothers. They are great hunters, and could bring home food for us all. They have no sister, so I could keep their lodge, and cook their food, and make their moccasins.'

Her grandmother thought that was a fine idea, so she helped Red Leaf select seven of her nicest robes, and seven pairs of her best moccasins. These she carried over to the lodge of the seven brothers.

The six brothers were hunting, and Moksois was down at the creek getting water when she came to the lodge, but she went in, anyway, and put one of the robes and a pair of moccasins on each of the seven beds. When he got back with the water, she was stirring the pot of soup on the fire. They talked and then he saw the robes and the moccasins.

'Where did these fine moccasins and robes come from?' he asked.

'I brought them. I thought it would be a good thing for us all if I became your sister,' Red Leaf answered, still stirring the soup.

'It suits me,' Moksois said. 'But I'll have to ask my brothers about it.'

When the brothers came home from the hunt and found the fine new robes and moccasins, and learned that Red Leaf wanted to be their sister, they thought it was a good arrangement.

So that was the way it was, from then on. They all lived together, very comfortably. The brothers hunted, and Red Leaf took care of the meat they brought home, and made their robes and moccasins, and Moksois helped by bringing in water, and keeping plenty of wood for fire.

But there came a day when everything was changed. Moksois took his bow and arrows and went out to hunt chipmunks. He wandered farther from the lodge than he thought. While he was gone, a giant buffalo bull came to the lodge and took Red Leaf and ran away with her.

He was the Double-Teethed Bull, strange mysterious bull, strongest of all the buffalo. He was different from the other buffalo, for he had teeth in his upper and in his lower jaw, and he ruled over them.

When Moksois returned to the lodge, he found it partly torn down, and the tracks of the great bull coming in and going out. He was very much afraid. Tears ran down his face while he searched for his sister. When he saw his brothers coming home from the hunt, he ran to them, crying, 'A great bull has stolen our sister.'

The brothers knew the tracks were those of a great Double-Teethed Bull. They began to mourn and cry. 'What can we do to save our sister? The Double-Teethed Bull is so powerful we can do nothing against him. He cannot be killed.'

At last, one said, 'We can't just sit here. Let's get busy and build four strong corrals[1] one inside the other. Then we'll go and try to get our sister away from him. That way, if we can get her, we will have some strong place to bring her.'

This they did, piling big logs together and bracing them like a fort. When all four were finished, little Moksois went out and gathered anthills and brought them back in his robe. He scattered the ants and sand in a line all around the inside of the smallest corral.

Then the seven brothers followed the tracks of their sister and the great bull for a long time. At last they came to the top of a high hill,

[1] a cattle enclosure made of log fencing.

from which they could look far across the plain. There they saw a great herd of buffalo, covering the plain as far as the eye could see. In the centre of the herd was a large open space, and in the open space sat their sister, with the great bull lying on the ground close by. No other buffalo were near them.

The brothers had brought their medicine sacks with them. One was made from the skin of a blackbird, one from that of a crow, one from a coyote skin, and one from the skin of a tiny yellow bird. Little Moksois' medicine sack was made of tanned buffalo hide, made in the shape of a half-moon, and he carried the skin of a gopher[1] inside it.

The eldest brother took the blackbird skin in his hand, and it changed into a live blackbird. He told the bird to fly down and try to get close enough to their sister to tell her they were there.

He flew close to Red Leaf, where she sat on the ground, half-covered by her robe. He tried to talk to her, but the great bull saw him there and rumbled, 'Blackbird, what are you trying to do? Are you a spy? Go away, or I will look at you and you will fall to the ground, dead.' The Blackbird was afraid of his power, so he flew back to the brothers.

The second brother sent the coyote that came alive from the coyote-skin medicine sack. The coyote was very clever. He slipped around far to the south, and came up on the other side of the herd. Then he went limping through the buffalo, acting as though he were sick and crippled.

But the Double-Teethed Bull was not fooled. He shook his heavy horns at him and said, 'Coyote, I think you are a spy. Go away, before I look at you and you die. . . .'

So Coyote was afraid to stay. He went back to the brothers. This time they tried the crow. He flew in close, lighting on the ground, and pecking as though gathering food, then flying a little closer and lighting again. But the bull suspected him. 'Go away, crow. Don't come any closer. You're trying to do something bad. I think I'll just look at you. Then you'll fall down dead. . . .' Crow didn't wait. He flew away, back to the brothers, waiting on the hill.

The last to go was the tiny yellow bird. He was so tiny that he crept

[1]a little prairie animal rather like a squirrel which nests in holes in the ground.

along through the grass, among the buffalo, without any of them seeing him, even the great bull. He slipped under Red Leaf's robe and said to her, 'Red Leaf, your brothers are yonder on the hill. They will try to save you. They sent me to tell you what to do. Just cover yourself all over with your robe, and pretend to go to sleep. Then wait.'

The great bull snorted, and rumbled in his throat, but he didn't see the little yellow bird as he crept back through the herd. When he got back to the hill the brothers took council among themselves. Moksois said, 'Now it is my turn to do something. Everyone be quiet. I will try to put the Double-Teethed Bull to sleep so we can do something.'

So he lay down on the ground with his half-moon medicine sack by his head and shut his eyes. Everyone kept very still, waiting. After a time he opened his eyes and arose. 'Blackbird, fly down and see if the bull is asleep,' he said.

When the blackbird came back, he said he'd seen the great bull sleeping soundly, with his nose against the ground.

'That is good,' said Moksois. 'I am to blame for the Double-Teethed Bull stealing our sister. Now I will get her back. All of you wait here, but be ready to run away when I get back.'

He opened his half-moon medicine sack and took the gopher skin out and laid it on the ground. Instantly, it became a live gopher, and started to dig with its long sharp claws. Moksois stayed right beside the gopher and followed it into the hole it was digging.

The gopher made a tunnel straight to where Red Leaf lay, covered by her robe. Moksois came up under the robe and took her by the hand and led her back along the gopher hole to where the brothers waited.

They took their sister, and as fast as they could, they ran toward home, to the shelter of the strong corrals they had built. But Moksois stayed behind, to keep watch on the herd. He wanted to see what happened when the great bull found Red Leaf gone. He felt very brave. 'I will stay here and watch,' he said. 'I am not afraid. Let the Double-Teethed Bull look at me. He can't kill me with one of his looks.'

The great bull heaved himself to his feet and shook himself all over. Then he walked over to Red Leaf's robe, still spread out on the ground over the gopher hole, and sniffed at it. When he saw she was gone, he bellowed and pawed the ground, throwing clouds of dust into the air. He tossed and hooked the robe with his sharp horns until he tore it to shreds.

All the buffalo were excited and milling around, pawing and bellowing. Then the bull saw the gopher hole. He sniffed at it then began to run back over the ground in the same direction Moksois and Red Leaf had gone through the tunnel. All the other buffalo followed him, charging at great speed; heads down, stirring up such a cloud of dust that it was like the smoke from a prairie fire.

Moksois watched them from the hill, but before they got too near, he put an arrow in his bow and shot it as far as he could, toward home. The instant the arrow touched the ground, Moksois was beside it. That was part of his power. He kept shooting his arrows until he reached the lodge.

'Get ready, the buffalo are coming,' he cried. And they all got inside the log corrals and kept watch. In a little while, the great herd of buffalo came in sight, galloping over the plain, with the huge bull out in front. When they saw the corrals, they stopped and waited while an old cow walked slowly nearer.

'Come back with me, Red Leaf. The Double-Teethed Bull wants you,' she called to them. 'If you don't return, he will come and get you himself.'

Moksois said, 'Tell him to come, if he dares.' But before she had gone very far, he shot the old cow, and she fell to the ground. Three other messengers came, asking Red Leaf to come back to the Double-Teethed Bull, and making threats. Each time Moksois gave them the same answer. Each time he shot them before they got back to the great bull. Only the last one got near enough to give him Moksois' message.

Then the great bull was terribly angry. He pranced and pawed. He hooked the ground and bellowed defiance. Head down, he charged the corral at a fast gallop, the herd thundering behind.

'Come out,' he roared to the girl. 'Come out. Don't you know who I am?'

Red Leaf was trembling and crying. She begged her brothers to let her go. 'He will kill you all. Let me go.... It may save you....'

But Moksois said, 'Don't be afraid. Don't cry. I will kill the bull.'

When the Double-Teethed Bull heard Moksois say that, he was furious. He charged the corral and hooked his horns in the logs, tossing them aside like sticks. The churning, bellowing herd charged the other corrals, one after another, scattering the logs like straws in the wind. But when they came to the place where Moksois had made the line inside with the anthills, every grain of sand had become a big rock, making a strong rock corral that stopped the buffalo charge.

Again and again the buffalo charged the wall, hurling the greatstones in every direction, like pebbles. The eldest brother said, 'Even these rocks can't stand against him. He will be inside, next time. . . .'

Their sister cried, 'Let me go . . . let me go outside, or he will kill you all.'

But Moksois said again, 'Don't be afraid. Stay here. I still have power. . . .' Then he shot his arrow straight up into the air, just as high as he could shoot it. And as high as it went, there stood a tall tree, reaching into the sky.

'Now, hurry, climb up there,' he cried, helping his sister into the tree. Quickly, all the brothers climbed up into the branches. But just as Moksois climbed to the lowest limb, the Double-Teethed Bull broke through the rocks with a terrible bellow that shook the hills.

He charged and charged the tree, tearing off great slivers with his sharp horns. But just as fast as he tossed a piece of wood aside it joined back to the tree the same as it had been before.

Moksois only waited to shoot his last arrow at the powerful bull, before he followed his brothers and his sister up and up the tree, until they went into the sky. There they became the seven stars. The girl is the head star, and the little one, off to one side by itself, is little Moksois, still keeping guard.

CHEYENNE INDIAN MYTH

Here are some passages taken from the spoken autobiography of an old Crow Indian Chief. Frank Linderman who was a journalist visited him on many occasions and persuaded him to tell the story of his life. Linderman then published this in 1908, so Chief Plenty-coups is talking about things as they were about 100 years ago.

Chief Plenty-coups tells the story of his life to Frank Linderman.

Memories of boyhood

'I was born eighty snows ago this summer (1848) at the place we call The-cliff-that-has-no-pass,' said Plenty-coups slowly. 'It is not far from the present site of Billings. My mother's name was Otter-woman. My father was Medicine-bird. I have forgotten the name of one of my grandmothers, but I remember her man's name, my grandfather's. It was Coyote-appears. My other grandmother, a Crow woman, married a man of the Shoshone. Her name was It-might-have-happened. She was my mother's mother.'

'What are your earliest remembrances?' I asked, feeling that I had interrupted him with my question.

He smiled, his pipe ready to light. 'Play,' he said happily. 'All boys are much alike. Their hearts are young, and they let them sing. We moved camp very often, and this to me, and the other boys of my age was great fun. As soon as the crier rode through the village telling the people to get ready to travel, I would find my young friends and we would catch up our horses as fast as the herders brought them in. Lodges[1] would come down quickly, horses would be packed, travois[2] loaded, and then away we would go to some new place we boys had never seen before. The long line of pack-horses and travois reaching farther than we could see, the dogs and bands of loose horses, all sweeping across the rolling plains or up a mountain trail to some mysterious destination, made our hearts sing with joy.'

The pleasure which thoughts of boyhood had brought to his face vanished now. His mind wandered from his story. 'My people were wise,' he said thoughtfully. 'They never neglected the young or failed to keep before

[1] Lodges: Indian tent.

[2] Travois: a kind of rack trailing behind a horse on which the Indians packed their possessions.

them deeds done by illustrious men of the tribe. Our teachers were willing and thorough. They were our grandfathers, fathers, or uncles. All were quick to praise excellence without speaking a word that might break the spirit of a boy who might be less capable than others. The boy who failed at any lesson got only more lessons, more care, until he was as far as he could go.'

'Your first lessons were with the bow and arrow?' I asked, to give him another start on his boyhood.

'Oh, no. Our first task was learning to run,' he replied, his face lighting up again. 'How well I remember my first lesson, and how proud I felt because my grandfather noticed me.'

The day was in summer, the world green and very beautiful. I was playing with some other boys when my grandfather stopped to watch. 'Take off your shirt and leggings,' he said to me.

I tore them from my back and legs, and, naked except for my moccasins, stood before him.

'Now catch me that yellow butterfly,' he ordered. 'Be quick!'

'Away I went after the yellow butterfly. How fast these creatures are, and how cunning! In and out among the trees and bushes, across streams, over grassy places, now low near the ground, then just above my head, the dodging butterfly led me far before I caught and held it in my hand. Panting but concealing my shortness of breath as best I could, I offered it to Grandfather, who whispered, as though he told me a secret, 'Rub its wings over your heart, my son, and ask the butterflies to lend you their grace and swiftness.'

'O Butterflies, lend me your grace and swiftness!' I repeated, rubbing the broken wings over my pouding heart. If this would give me grace and speed I should catch many butterflies. I knew. But instead of keeping the secret I told my friends, as my grandfather knew I would,' Plenty-coups chuckled, 'and how many, many we boys caught after that to rub over our hearts. We chased butterflies to give us endurance in running, always rubbing our breasts with their wings, asking the butterflies to give us a portion of their power. We worked very hard at this, because running is necessary both in hunting and in war. I was never the swiftest among my friends, but not many could run farther than I.'

'Is running a greater accomplishment than swimming?' I asked.

'Yes,' he answered, 'but swimming is more fun. In all seasons of the year most men were in the rivers before sunrise. Boys had plenty of teachers here. Sometimes they were hard on us, too. They would often send us into the water to swim among cakes of floating ice and the ice taught us to take care of our bodies. Cold toughens a man. The buffalo-runners, in winter, rubbed their hands with sand and snow to prevent their fingers from stiffening in using the bow and arrow.

Crow Indian

'Perhaps we could all be in our fathers' lodges by the fire when some teacher would call, 'Follow me, and do as I do!' Then we would run outside to follow him, racing behind him to the bank of a river. On the very edge he would turn a flip-flop into the water. Every boy who failed at the flip-flop was thrown in and ducked. The flip-flop was difficult for me. I was ducked many times before I learned it.

'We were eager to learn from both the men and the beasts who excelled in anything, and so never got through learning. But swimming was most fun, and therefore we worked harder at this than at other tasks. Whenever a boy's father caught a beaver, the boy got the tail and brought it to us. We would take turns slapping our joints and muscles with the flat beaver's tail until they burned under our blows. 'Teach us your power in the water, O Beaver!' we said, making our skins smart with the tail.'

'One morning after I was eight years old we were called together by my grandfather. He had killed a grizzly bear the day before, and when we gathered near him I saw that he held the grizzly's heart in his hand. We all knew well what was expected of us, since every Crow warrior has eaten some of the heart of a grizzly bear, so that he may truthfully say, 'I have the heart of a grizzly!' I say this, even to this day, when there is trouble to face, and the words help me to keep my head. They clear my mind, make me suddenly calm.'

'One day when the chokecherries were black and the plums red on the trees, my grandfather rode through the village, calling twenty of us older boys by name. The buffalo-runners had been out since daybreak, and we guessed what was before us. 'Get on your horses and follow me,' said my grandfather, riding out on the plains.

'We rode fast. Nothing was in sight until Grandfather led us over a hill. There we saw a circle of horsemen about one hundred yards across, and in its centre a huge buffalo bull. We knew he had been wounded and tormented until he was very dangerous, and when we saw him there defying the men on horseback we began to dread the ordeal that was at hand.

The circle parted as we rode through it, and the bull, angered by the stir we made, charged and sent us flying. The men were laughing at us when we returned, and this made me feel very small. They had again surrounded the bull, and I now saw an arrow sticking deep in his side. Only its feathers were sticking out of a wound that dripped blood on the ground.

'Get down from your horses, young men,' said my grandfather. 'A cool head with quick feet, may strike this bull on the root of his tail with a bow. Be lively, and take care of yourselves. The young man who strikes, and is himself not hurt, may count coup.'

I was first off my horse. Watching the bull, I slipped out of shirt and leggings, letting them fall where I stood. Naked, with only my bow in my right hand, I stepped away from my clothes, feeling that I might never see them again. I was not quite nine years old.

The bull saw me, a human being afoot! He seemed to know that now he might kill, and he began to paw the ground and bellow as I walked carefully toward him.

Suddenly he stopped pawing, and his voice was still. He came to meet me, his eyes green with anger and pain, I saw blood dropping from his side, not red blood now, but mixed with yellow.

I stopped walking and stood still. This seemed to puzzle the bull, and he too stopped in his tracks. We looked at each other, the sun hot on my naked back. Heat from the plains danced on the bull's horns and head; his sides were panting, and his mouth was bloody.

I knew that the men were watching me. I could feel their eyes on my back. I must go on. One step, two steps. The grass was soft and thick under my feet. Three steps. 'I am a Crow. I have the heart of a grizzly bear,' I said to myself. Three steps more. And then he charged!

A cheer went up out of a cloud of dust. I had struck the bull on the root of his tail! But I was in even greater danger than before.

Two other boys were after the bull now, but in spite of them he turned and came at me. To run was foolish. I stood still, waiting. The bull stopped very near me and bellowed, blowing bloody froth from his nose. The other boys, seeing my danger, did not move. The bull was not more than four bows' lengths from me, and I could feel my heart beating like a war-drum.

Two large gray wolves crossed the circle just behind him, but the bull did not notice them, did not move an eye. He saw only me, and I was growing tired from the strain of watching him. I must get relief, must tempt him to come on. I stepped to my right. Instantly he charged—but I had dodged back to my left, across his way, and I struck him when he passed. This time I ran among the horsemen, with a lump of bloody froth on my breast. I had had enough.'

At the end of this book of the Life of Chief Plenty-coups Frank Linderman wrote the following:

Plenty-coups refused to speak of his life after the passing of the buffalo, so that his story seems to have been broken off, leaving many years unaccounted for. 'I have not told you half that happened when I was young,' he said, when urged to go on. 'I can think back and tell you much more of war and horse stealing. But when the buffalo went away the hearts of my people fell to the ground, and they could not lift them up again. After this nothing happened. There was little singing anywhere. Besides,' he added sorrowfully, 'you know that part of my life as well as I do. You saw what happened to us when the buffalo went away.'

I do know that part of his life's story, and that part of the lives of all the Indians of the Northwestern plains; and I did see what happened to these sturdy, warlike people when the last of the buffalo was finally slaughtered and left to decay on the plains by skin-hunting white men.

From *Plenty-Coups; Chief of the Crows.* FRANK LINDERMAN

For discussion and writing

The story of Moksois and the Double-teethed Buffalo would make a good play or dance drama (see Appendix 9).

The prairies are very wide, and the sky seems enormous and the stars very bright. The Indians lived in tents and were constantly on the move, so the night sky was naturally something they enquired about.

Try writing a story of this sort which gives a non-scientific explanation of something in the world around you.

Among the Crow Indians, when a warrior did a particularly daring act, he could 'count coup' or score a point of honour as it were. If he had never managed to 'count coup' he could not marry until he was 25 years old. As his name suggests Plenty-coups had been a very daring man who became a Chief. *Have we in England any ways of scoring points of honour?*

What do you think of the Indian methods of teaching their children to run and swim and hunt?

What kind of things have you learned from your father and uncles and other grown-up relatives?

Do you think your family and friends could teach you all you need to know?

If it were possible would you prefer to be educated at home?

The story of his life which Plenty-coups told was a spoken autobiography which Frank Linderman wrote down as he spoke it.

In pairs, with one acting as the interviewer and note taker, begin to tell the story of your life so far.

Bear mask from the north west coast of America.

Animals played an important part in the Indians' lives. They hunted them, but they also loved them and believed they could share their characteristics. At times they felt they were indeed wolves, bears, otters; similarly, a bear or an otter might turn out to be an Otter-Person or a Bear-Person.

Write a story in which you become an Animal-Person—whatever animal you like.

Which of the stories about a buffalo do you like best—the myth of Moksois and the Great Bull, or Plenty-coups' memories of facing the wounded buffalo?

If you are interested in myths write one whose events and characters belong to an area you know well;

or if there is any incident in your own life in which you had an encounter with an animal which frightened you, write about it; or write a story called The Great Beast.

The Indians always hoped the buffaloes would come back. They could not understand that they had gone for ever.

How and why were the buffaloes destroyed?

The next three pieces—a piece of history, a folk song and a poem, tell you the answer.

The Slaughter of the Buffalo

The buffalo skinner set out upon one of the most strange and savage enterprises that Americans have ever undertaken. When the white man reached the great plains, he found in the Plains Indian an antagonist he could not defeat. These Indians lived a nomadic life, following the buffalo herds, and so long as these herds lasted, the mounted and hard-fighting aborigines could not be cornered and starved out. The plains were vast and the herds of buffalo were so large that they turned the prairie black for as far as a man could see. One frontiersman speaks of a herd that stretched for 'seven miles from the Arkansas river to the foot-hills . . . a living mass of buffalo, pressing in countless thousands upon each other . . . a migration of millions of prime animals.' Another plainsman tells of an even larger herd: 'For five days we rode through and camped in a mobile sea of buffalo.' Perhaps this was the same herd that was said to have drunk the Arkansas River dry. Every season these armies of bison migrated from the plains of Texas north to Hudson Bay and back, with the Indians always on their flanks, taking what they needed for their year's supply of meat.

The United States Government entered the picture by declaring a bounty on buffalo hides and the slaughter began. Parties of Buffalo hunters—two to shoot, four to skin, one to cook—swarmed over the plains. The sluggish and stupid animals were easy to kill. Upwind, a man could lie at his ease on a hillock and knock over as many as seventy-five or a hundred with as many shots from his long range rifle.

Soon tens of thousands of raw and grisly bodies littered the plains and the arroyos, food for the wolves and the buzzards, but not for the Indians. The hides, hauled to the railroad and shipped East, began to command a good price as rugs and as women's coats. The slaughter continued, with exhibitionists like Buffalo Bill running the show and with the railroads taking trainloads of hunters out on the prairies to kill more thousands of the beasts for sport. Old-timers can remember places in the West where you could walk for a mile on the skeletons without ever having to step on the ground. Years later, these bones, bleached white by the wind and the rain, were sold for fertilizer, bringing more money to the bone-hunters than the buffalo skinners had ever obtained.

The toughest of old-time cowboys shunned the buffalo hunters and their Texas capital, the god-forsaken little town of Jacksboro. They claimed that 'if them buffalo hunters don't kill ye for money, they'll try to kill ye for meanness.' This ballad is a testament to their ruthlessness. A former buffalo hunter, who claims to have been in the party when old Crego got his, gave the senior editor the following account of the incident. . . .

'It was a hell of a trip down Pease River, lasting several months. We fought sandstorms, flies, bedbugs, wolves, and Indians. At the end of the season old Crego announced he had lost money and could not pay us off. We argued the question with him.

He didn't see our side of things, so we shot him down and left his damned old bones to bleach where we had left so many stinking buffalo. On the way back to Jacksboro, one of the boys started up a song about the trip and the hard times and old Crego and we all set in to help him. Before we got back to Jacksboro we had shaped it up and the whole crowd could sing it.'

ALAN LOMAX

The Buffalo Skinners

'Twas in the town of Jacksboro in the year of '73,
When a man by the name of Crego came stepping up to me,
Saying. 'How do you do, young fellow, and how would you
like to go
And spend one summer pleasantly on the range of the buffalo?'

It's me being out of employment, boys, to old Crego I did say,
'This going out on the buffalo range depends upon the pay.
But if you will pay good wages, give transportation, too,
I think, sir, I will go with you to the range of the buffalo.'

It's now our outfit was complete, seven able-bodied men.
With navy six and needle gun our troubles did begin;
Our way, it was a pleasant one, the route we had to go,
Until we crossed Pease River on the range of the buffalo.

It's now we've crossed Pease River, our troubles have begun,
The first damned tail I went to rip, it's how I cut my thumb!
The water was salty as hell-fire, the beef I could not go,
And the Indians waited to pick us off, while skinning the buffalo.

Our hearts were cased with buffalo hocks, our souls were
cased with steel,
And the hardships of that summer would nearly make us reel.

While skinning the damned old stinkers, our lives they had no show,
For the Indians waited to pick us off on the hills of Mexico.

The season being near over, boys, old Crego, he did say
The crowd had been extravagant, was in debt to him that day.
We coaxed him and we begged him, but still it was no go—
So we left his damned old bones to bleach on the range of
the buffalo.

Oh, it's now we've crossed Pease River and homeward we
are bound.
No more in that hell-fired country shall ever we be found
Go home to our wives and sweethearts, tell others not to go.
For God's foresaken the buffalo range and the damned old buffalo.

Popular song of the 1870's

The Flower-fed Buffaloes

The flower-fed buffaloes of the spring
In the days of long ago,
Ranged where the locomotives sing
And the prairie flowers lie low:-
The tossing, blooming perfumed grass,
Is swept away by the wheat,
Wheels and wheels and wheels spin by
In the spring that still is sweet.
But the flower-fed buffaloes of the spring
Left us, long ago.
They gore no more, they bellow no more,
They trundle around the hills no more:
With the Blackfeet, lying low,
With the Pawness, lying low,
Lying low.

VACHEL LINDSAY

For discussion and writing

There was warfare between the white frontiersmen and Indians all through the eighteen hundreds until the white men realised that the lives of the Indians and buffaloes were so intertwined that the only way to conquer the Indians would be to destroy the buffaloes. This they did.

Looked at from today, does this seem to be a good thing to have done?

Do you think your point of view might have been different if you had lived at the time?

Write a story about a family of white settlers who have just started to farm on the prairie frontier, either from the point of view of the white men or of the Indians who have lived on this same prairie for as long as they can remember.

Why do you think Plenty-coups would not tell about his life after the disappearance of the buffaloes?

Write about any great change in your life, such as a move from the country to the town; or from another country to England. Say what you miss in the old life and like in the new.

Collect some stories from older people about what it was like when things were different; such things as harvesting before the days of the combine-harvester, the days of oil lamps and candles, cooking on coal burning fires and kitchen stoves, going to work at fourteen, or even thirteen—and any other stories you can persuade people to tell you.

The account by the old Buffalo Hunter tells how this ballad came to be made up. It arose out of an incident of anger and violence.

In groups, or as a class, try to compose a balled arising from some violent incident of today. (See Appendix 7, where there is a boy's ballad about a heroic figure).

Read The Flower-fed Buffaloes *aloud. Try using groups of readers for different parts of the poem. Discuss what mood you want the voices to express. Try to find a record of some music that matches its mood, and play this before you read it.*

Make a documentary programme called Buffalo *for radio using short passages of the prose and poems in this section. You might link the passages by appropriate music. About 20 minutes might be a good length for it. You will need to rehearse it several times. (See Appendix 4 'Arranging a Programme'.)*

NO BOUNDARIES

10. Jokers

A a

B b

H h

P p

Peter Piper's Practical Principles of Plain and Perfect Pronunciation

PETER PIPER'S POLITE PREFACE

Peter Piper Puts Pen to Paper, to Produce his Peerless Production, Proudly Presuming it will Please Princes, Peers, and Parliaments, and Procure him the Praise and Plaudits of their Progeny and Posterity, as he can prove it Positively to be a PARAGON, or Playful, Palatable, Proverbial, Panegyrical, Philosophical, Philanthropical Phænomenon of Productions.

A a

Andrew Airpump ask'd his Aunt her Ailment:
Did Andrew Airpump ask his Aunt her Ailment?
If Andrew Airpump ask'd his aunt her Ailment,
Where was the Ailment of Andrew Airpump's Aunt?

B b

Billy Button bought a butter'd Biscuit:
Did Billy Button buy a butter'd Biscuit?
If Billy Button bought a butter'd Biscuit,
Where's the butter'd biscuit Billy Button bought?

H h

Humphrey Hunchback had a Hundred Hedgehogs:
Did Humphrey Hunchback have a hundred Hedgehogs?
If Humphrey Hunchback had a Hundred Hedgehogs,
Where's the Hundred Hedgehogs Humphrey Hunchback had?

P p

Peter Piper pick'd a Peck of Pepper:- - -

Q q

Quixote Quicksight quiz'd a queerish Quidbox:- - -

W w

Walter Waddle won a walking Wager:- - -

X x Y y Z z

X Y Z have made my Brains to crack-o,
X smokes, Y snuffs, and Z chews tobacco;
Yet oft by X Y Z much learning's taught;
But Peter Piper beats them all to nought.

From *Flowers of Delight.* *Ed.* LEONARD DE VRIES

X x Y y Z z

These tongue-twisters come from an old book for children.

Try making up some of the missing verses of this tongue-twisting alphabet.

Try reading these verses aloud in groups of four or five.

Make a collection of any crazy rhymes you know; arrange a short performance with small groups of people each reciting (or reading) a different one.

Here is an outrageous ballad together with the true incident it was based on.

Little Billee

There were three sailors of Bristol city
  Who took a boat and went to sea.
But first with beef and captain's biscuits
  And pickled pork they loaded she.

There was gorging Jack and guzzling Jimmy,
  And the youngest he was little Billee.
Now when they got as far as the Equator
  They'd nothing left but one split pea.

Says gorging Jack to guzzling Jimmy,
  'I am extremely hungaree.'
To gorging Jack says guzzling Jimmy,
  'We've nothing left, us must eat we.'

Says gorging Jack to guzzling Jimmy,
  'With one another we shouldn't agree!
There's little Bill, he's young and tender,
  We're old and tough, so let's eat he.'

'Oh! Billy, we're going to kill and eat you,
  So undo the button of your chemie.'
When Bill received this information
  He used his pocket handkerchie.

'First let me say my catechism,
  Which my poor mammy taught to me.'
'Make haste, make haste,' says guzzling Jimmy,
  While Jack pulled out his snickersnee.

So Billy went up to the main-top gallant mast,
And down he fell on his bended knee.
He scarce had come to the twelfth commandment
When up he jumps. 'There's land I see:

'Jerusalem and Madagascar,
And North and South Amerikee:
There's the British flag a riding at anchor,
With Admiral Napier, K.C.B.'

So when they got aboard of the Admiral's
He hanged fat Jack and flogged Jimmee:
But as for little Bill, he made him
The Captain of a Seventy-three.

WILLIAM MAKEPEACE THACKERAY

Providential Escape

Some few years since, a ship at sea, caught fire, the whole crew of which was obliged to take to their boat. After beating about for many days in the ocean, having only a large blanket for a sail; their whole stock of provisions being gone, and sorely pressed by hunger, they came to the resolution of casting lots, which of them should first be killed for supplying the others with food. The lot happened to fall upon one who was greatly beloved by the whole of the crew; and then who should take his life away became another difficulty, it was, however, at last determined to bleed him to death: but, at the very instant the fatal incision was about to be made, one of the company espied a sail at a great distance. It proved to be a merchant-ship from England, which took in the unhappy sufferers, and brought most of them safe to land.

A gentleman's coach, with an arms and crest painted thereon, describing this story, with a very appropriate motto, used frequently, to pass to and fro, in the city of London, about the year 1772.

Most people laugh at this ballad yet the actual incident must have been appalling for the sailors at the time.

Write a crazy story or ballad about cannibals, or ghosts, or an explosion or a death by poison, or any dreadful incident that takes your fancy.

Describe the most extraordinary person you have ever seen.

Write a story in which you see this character and follow him (or her). What happened?

Why do you think the Gentleman referred to on p. 170 chose this incident and the motto 'From Fire, Water and Famine by Providence Preserved' for his coat of arms?

Write the story behind this.

The Surprising Adventures of Bamfylde Moore Carew

Bamfylde Moore Carew was the son of a Devonshire clergyman who lived in the first part of the 18th century. His family was well-known and wealthy and he was given a splendid christening, which all the ladies and gentlemen of rank and quality in the West of England attended. When he was twelve he was sent to Blundell's school at Tiverton and up until he was about sixteen he was a model pupil and worked so hard at his Latin and Greek that everyone thought he would go to the University and become a clergyman like his father. But he worked very hard at something else besides Latin and Greek and that was hunting. The boys at Tiverton school had their own pack of hounds; Bamfylde was strong and handsome and energetic and he used to run with the hounds and cheer them on in a great ringing voice. He got to know farmers and gypsies and he found out a secret, which he kept to himself, of enticing any dog to follow him. On one occasion, just before harvest time, he led the hounds on a hot chase for many miles, and did so much damage to the fields of corn that the farmers complained very angrily to the Headmaster and demanded that the ringleaders be punished. The threats and the row were so great that Bamfylde and three of his schoolmates absented themselves from school. In the evening they went to a country alehouse where they fell in with a group of a dozen or so gypsies who happened to be there drinking and singing. Bamfylde and his friends joined their party and stayed for a feast and dancing afterwards.

They liked the gypsies so much that they declared their intention of joining them. Considering their birth and education and appearance the gypsies thought they were joking, but when the boys stayed all night and in the morning were still of the same mind, the gypsies believed them and said they could become members of their society. But first they had to go through a proper ceremony and take oaths to the gypsy king and promise to keep the rules of the gypsy people.

Bamfylde loved the life and he first gained a reputation as a dog stealer because of his power to entice dogs away from their owners. One of his early adventures concerned some buried treasure. Gypsies are supposed to have magical powers, and in particular to be able to foretell the future. A lady living near Taunton in Somerset consulted him about a large quantity of money which she was convinced was buried somewhere in the grounds of her house. She promised to reward him handsomely if he could tell her where to find it. Bamfylde consulted 'his secret art and after long toil and study' told the lady that the treasure lay under a laurel-tree in the garden, but that she must wait until her planet of fortune was in a favourable position in the heavens in three months time; until then she was not to start digging. The lady was delighted with this information and paid him twenty guineas. However, perhaps Bamfylde was not experienced enough in the arts of the gypsies, or perhaps the lady mistook her lucky hour, but she did not find the treasure, and by that time Bamfylde was in another part of the country.

His interest and skill with animals led him to seek out an expert rat-catcher whom he paid handsomely to teach him his secrets which included curing madness in dogs or cattle. All these things he could do as a gypsy, but because he was an educated gentleman he always had to disguise himself, and he soon began to take on all sorts of different characters.

In the days of sail, shipwreck was always a possibility and in the West of England everyone was familiar with the sight of destitute sailors begging their way to their homes or to a port where they might find another ship. So the first disguise he tried was that of a shipwrecked seaman. He put on an old pair of trousers, a ragged jacket, leaking shoes and a black woollen cap. He changed his manners with his dress, forgot his family, education and politeness, and became for the time an unfortunate, ignorant seaman, but he had to forge the passes and certificates which you had to have if you were to be allowed to beg your way from one part of the country to another.

Having dressed himself as a seaman he walked down to Exeter Quay and in a rough and direct manner asked to speak to a Customs Officer. He told this Customs man that he had come from France in a ship that was running a cargo of smuggled goods and that the captain was a villain and had treated him so badly he was going to be revenged on him. The Customs man swallowed all he said with greedy ears and took him into the Customs house, gave him a bumper of cherry brandy, and then persuaded him to wet the other eye with another bumper of the same. Clearly they thought the more he drank the more he would tell them about the smuggled goods. They even asked him if he wanted money. But he was too clever to say yes and replied he had no mercenary motives; he only wanted to be revenged on his captain. So they took him to the Boot Inn in Exeter. A fire was lighted in a private room upstairs and a couple of roasted ducks and glasses of wine and punch went round and they insisted on pressing four guineas into his hand. Whereupon he began to talk with great freedom, gave a particular account of the vessel, where they had taken their cargo in France, what it consisted of, the day they had sailed and finally admitted that they had landed the valuable cargo and concealed much of it in the outhouses of Squire Mallock of Cockington near Torquay, and the remainder in the outhouses of Squire Cary of Tor-abbey. Both these houses were very near the sea.

The Customs Officers having now got the scent were like hounds wanting to be off on the chase, and they insisted that the sailor should come with them. But a seaman with Kings men would be suspicious so they gave him different clothes—a ruffled shirt, a fine suit of broadcloth belonging to the Customs Collector himself, and a gold laced hat—then mounting him on a fine black mare, away they rode together, being eight of them.

They reached Newton-Bushel by nightfall and slept at the Bull Inn. Nothing was wanting to make the night jovial; rich food and wine and music afterwards. The Customs Officers were already enjoying in imagination all the booty they would confiscate the next day. Thinking they could not do enough for the honest sailor, they asked if he knew anything of accounts; if he did, they said, he could have a job in the Customs.

In the morning after a hearty breakfast, they set out for Tor-abbey. When they got to Torquay they sought out the constable and demanded his help in their search. Somewhat to their surprise, he was very unwilling. He said Squire Cary was beloved by everyone and that anyone who did anything to make him uneasy would be very unpopular. However, in the end the constable went along with the Customs party.

When they came to Tor-abbey they all dismounted, and the Customs

Officer asked the sailor to hold his horse, but the sailor replied that he knew the house and grounds and he would go round the gardens and meet them on the other side of the house to prevent anything being rushed away on that side. Since he knew where it had all been hidden he would be able to forestall any attempts to get it away when the alarm was given.

This seemed quite right to the Collector who fastened his horse to the garden rails and proceeded with his men to search the kennels, coal-house, dove-house, stables and all other likely outhouses, expecting every minute to see the informing sailor, who by this time had nearly got back to Newton-Bushel. He stopped at the Bull where they had been the preceding night, and drank a bottle of wine; then, having ordered a handsome dinner to be got ready for the rest of his companions whom he said he had had to leave because urgent business called him to Exeter, he clapped spurs to his horse and galloped the twenty odd miles to the Oxford Inn at Exeter where he and his friends were well known to the landlord. He told the landlord he was now a reformed character and lived at home respectably. He spent the night very jovially calling for the best of everything. In the morning he asked the landlord to do him the favour of lending him a couple of guineas till he could get some money from a merchant in the city. As the landlord had the Collector's valuable mare in his stables he was quite willing to do this. Bamfylde then quietly left the Inn without saying he was going, and went to the house where the gypsies used to meet when they were in that city. Here, he pulled off the fine clothes the Collector had lent him, rigged himself out again in a seaman's jacket and trousers and set off for Topsham, about three miles down river from Exeter, and a port of some size. Here he played the same trick on the Officer there, informing them of great smuggling concealments at Sir Copplestone Bamfylde's house north east of Exeter for which they rewarded him with a fine meal and a couple of guineas.

Meanwhile the Exeter Customs Officers having searched all the outhouses at Squire Cary's and found nothing, began to suspect the sailor had outwitted them, so they returned in a great hurry to Newton-Bushel. Soon after they had dismounted the landlord brought them the splendid dinner that Bamfylde had ordered for them. However, they were too vexed and angry to enjoy it; besides they had to pay for it, and when they got to Exeter they were told that the Collector's horse was at the Oxford Inn and they had to pay for Bamfylde's lodging there and the money he had borrowed, so they were very angry. From Topsham Bamfylde went to Exmouth where he played the same trick, always being just in advance of any news of his doings and from there he worked his way up the coast to Lyme Regis, Weymouth and Poole. This particular series of adventures was brought to an end when he was lying down to take a nap (having drunk too freely) in the bedroom of an Inn in Poole Harbour. Through the wall he heard some people talking and drinking in the next room. They were describing with much laughter the great confusion there was in all the seaports of the West of England owing to the tricks played on the Customs Officers by Bamfylde Carew. Hearing this, Bamfylde judged

Poole was no place for him to stay in, so he jumped up, went out by a back door and with much difficulty climbed over the garden wall and was away to Christchurch in Hampshire where he became once again a tattered, begging shipwrecked seaman. There were so many such sailors that it was the safest disguise for him to assume.

Bamfylde, of course, enjoyed his extraordinary life and his fame as a trickster. No one knew what disguise he would turn up in next, and any beggar who knocked at the door might be him. Wealthy country gentlemen laid bets with each other that he would not deceive them, but he usually did. One of his favourite tricks was to call on the aristocratic friends of his family, wheedle some money out of them, and then declare who he was, and usually then, he was invited to stay for a few days and treated handsomely.

When he grew old he gave up being the King of the Gypsies and retired to the West of England where he bought a neat cottage and lived in a manner becoming to a good old English gentleman, respected by his neighbours and beloved by the poor, to whom his doors were ever open.

Adapted from *The Surprising Adventures of Bamfylde Moore Carew*

Write a further surprising adventure for Bamfylde Moore Carew.
Here are some suggestions to start you off:

How he disguised himself as a poor widow woman with a borrowed child whom he had trained to say 'drowned in the boat; drowned in the boat'.

How he stole 5 dogs from an unfriendly parson who would not give him anything to eat or drink.

How he was arrested for begging and thrown into prison; and how he escaped.

How he pretended to be a blind beggar.

An adventure arising from telling fortunes.

Write a story about a gypsy.

Expand any part of the story of Bamfylde's life that interests you.

Find some poems or ballads about gypsies and arrange them as a programme for reading aloud. You might introduce and conclude this programme by suitable music.

Have you ever had your fortune told by a fortune teller? Write about this.

Many people dislike gypsies very much. If you have ever come across any, write an account of them.

Taking the Mickey

Every underdog, including children, enjoys stories about upsetting people at the top.

Here are two stories about animals,—but are they really about animals?

The Lion, the Hyena, and the Jackal

Game being rare, the lion invited the hyena and the jackal to hunt with him on a certain summer day.

The association proved to be fruitful; in a short while the ground was strewn with antelopes and gazelles. A lavish meal awaited the hunters. The lion, fair by nature, asked the hyena to divide the shares. The latter, with his powerful jaws, soon cut up the game into pieces, and made three obviously equal piles. 'Very good,' said the lion when the work was finished, 'but what is the meaning of these piles?'

'This one,' said the hyena, 'is for you, that one for me, and the other one for the jackal.'

Two powerful blows with his paws, knocking over the hyena, constituted the first reaction of the lion, who then explained: 'That is no way to divide the shares; people are right to say that you are dense.'

The lion calmed himself and said to the jackal: 'See if you can settle this question.'

The jackal restored the piles of meat, which had been scattered by the lion, and said: 'This first pile is for you, the second pile is for your meal tonight, and the third pile is for your lunch tomorrow.'

The lion was extremely pleased. 'Who taught you to divide shares like that?'

'It was the cuff you gave to the hyena,' said the jackal.

Tuareg story

The White Rabbit Caper

As the Boys who turn out the Mystery Programmes on the Air might write a story for Children

Fred Fox was pouring himself a slug of rye when the door of his office opened and in hopped old Mrs Rabbit. She was a white rabbit with pink eyes, and she wore a shawl on her head, and gold-rimmed spectacles.

'I want you to find Daphne,' she said tearfully, and she handed Fred Fox a snapshot of a white rabbit with pink eyes that looked to him like a picture of every other white rabbit with pink eyes.

'When did she hop the hutch?' asked Fred Fox.

'Yesterday,' said old Mrs Rabbit. 'She is only eighteen months old, and I am afraid that some superstitious creature has killed her for one of her feet.'

Fred Fox turned the snapshot over and put it in his pocket. 'Has this bunny got a throb?' he asked.

'Yes,' said old Mrs Rabbit. 'Franz Frog, repulsive owner of the notorious Lily Pad Night Club.'

Fred Fox leaped to his feet. 'Come on, Grandma,' he said, 'and don't step on your ears. We got to move fast.'

On the way to the Lily Pad Night Club, old Mrs Rabbit scampered so fast that Fred Fox had all he could do to keep up with her. 'Daphne is my great-great-great-great-great-granddaughter, if my memory serves,' said old Mrs Rabbit. 'I have thirty-nine thousand descendants.'

'This isn't going to be easy,' said Fred Fox. 'Maybe you should have gone to a magician with a hat.'

'But she is the only one named Daphne,' said old Mrs Rabbit, 'and she lived alone with me on my great carrot farm.'

They came to a broad brook. 'Skip it!' said Fred Fox.

'Keep a civil tongue in your head, young man,' snapped old Mrs Rabbit.

Just as they got to the Lily Pad, a dandelion clock struck twelve noon. Fred Fox pushed the button on the great green door, on which was painted a white water lily. The door opened an eighth of an inch, and Ben Rat peered out. 'Beat it,' he said, but Fred Fox shoved the door open, and old Mrs Rabbit followed him into a cool green hallway, softly but restlessly lighted by thousands of fireflies imprisoned in the hollow crystal pendants of an enormous chandelier. At the right there was a flight of green-carpeted stairs, and at the bottom of the steps the door to the cloakroom. Straight ahead, at the end of the long hallway, was the cool green door to Franz Frog's office.

'Beat it,' said Ben Rat again.

'Talk nice,' said Fred Fox, 'or I'll seal your house up with tin. Where's the Croaker?'

Once a gumpaw, always a gumpaw,' grumbled Ben Rat. 'He's in his office.'

'With Daphne?'

'Who's Daphne?' asked Ben Rat.

'My great-great-great-great-great-granddaughter,' said old Mrs Rabbit.

'Nobody's that great,' snarled Ben Rat.

Fred Fox opened the cool green door and went into Franz Frog's office, followed by old Mrs Rabbit and Ben Rat, The owner of the Lily Pad sat behind his desk, wearing a green suit, green shirt, green tie, green socks, and green shoes. He had an emerald tiepin and seven emerald rings. 'Whong you wong, Fonnxx?' he rumbled in a cold, green, cavernous voice. His eyes bulged and his throat began to swell ominously.

'He's going to croak,' explained Ben Rat.

'Nuts,' said Fred Fox, 'He'll outlive all of us.'

'Glunk,' croaked Franz Frog.

Ben Rat glared at Fred Fox. 'You oughta go on the stage,' he snarled.

'Where's Daphne?' demanded Fred Fox.

'Hoong Dangneng?' asked Franz Frog.

'Your bunny friend,' said Fred Fox.

'Nawng,' said Franz Frog.

Fred Fox picked up a cello in a corner and put it down. It was too light to contain a rabbit. The front-door bell rang. 'I'll get it,' said Fred Fox. It was Oliver (Hoot) Owl, a notorious fly-by-night. 'What're you doing up at this hour, Hoot?' asked Fred Fox.

'I'm trying to blind myself, so I'll confess,' said Hoot Owl testily.

'Confess to what?' snapped Fred Fox.

'What can't you solve?' asked Hoot Owl.

'The disappearance of Daphne,' said Fred Fox.

'Who's Daphne?' asked Hoot Owl.

Franz Frog hopped out of his office into the hall. Ben Rat and old Mrs Rabbit followed him.

Down the steps from the second floor came Sherman Stork, carrying a white muffler or something and grinning foolishly.

'Well, bless my soul!' said Fred Fox. 'If it isn't old midhusband himself! What did you do with Daphne?'

'Who's Daphne?' asked Sherman Stork.

'Fox thinks somebody killed Daphne Rabbit,' said Ben Rat.

'Fonnxx cung brong,' rumbled Franz Frog.

'I *could* be wrong,' said Fred Fox, 'but I'm not.' He pulled open the cloakroom door at the bottom of the steps, and the dead body of a female white rabbit toppled furrily on to the cool green carpet. Her head had been bashed in by a heavy blunt instrument.

'Daphne!' screamed old Mrs Rabbit, bursting into tears.

'I can't see a thing,' said Hoot Owl.

'It's a dead white rabbit,' said Ben Rat. 'Anybody can see that. You're dumb.'

'I'm wise!' said Hoot Owl indignantly. 'I know everything.'

'Jeeng Crine,' moaned Franz Frog. He stared up at the chandelier, his eyes bulging and his mammoth mouth gaping open. All the fireflies were frightened and went out.

The cool green hallway became pitch dark. There was a shriek in the black, and a feathery 'plump'. The fireflies lighted up to see what had happened. Hoot Owl lay dead on the cool green carpet, his head bashed in by a heavy blunt instrument. Ben Rat, Franz Frog, Sherman Stork, old Mrs Rabbit, and Fred Fox stared at Hoot Owl. Over the cool green carpet crawled a warm red stain, whose source was the body of Hoot Owl. He lay like a feather duster.

'Murder!' squealed old Mrs Rabbit.

'Nobody leaves this hallway!' snapped Fred Fox. 'There's a killer loose in this club!'

'I am not used to death,' said Sherman Stork.

'Roong!' groaned Franz Frog.

'He says he's ruined,' said Ben Rat, but Fred Fox wasn't listening. He was looking for a heavy blunt instrument. There wasn't any.

'Search them!' cried old Mrs Rabbit. 'Somebody has a sap, or a sock full of sand, or something!'

'Yeh,' said Fred Fox. 'Ben Rat is a sap—maybe someone swung him by his tail.'

'You oughta go on the stage,' snarled Ben Rat.

Fred Fox searched the suspects, but he found no concealed weapon.

'You could have strangled them with that muffler,' Fred Fox told Sherman Stork.

'But they were not strangled,' said Sherman Stork.

Fred Fox turned to Ben Rat. 'You could have bitten them to death with your ugly teeth,' he said.

'But they weren't bitten to death,' said Ben Rat.

Fred Fox stared at Franz Frog. 'You could have scared them to death with your ugly face,' he said.

'Bung wung screng to deng,' said Franz Frog.

'You're right,' admitted Fred Fox. 'They weren't. Where's old Mrs Rabbit?' he asked suddenly.

'I'm hiding in here,' called old Mrs Rabbit from the cloakroom. 'I'm frightened.'

Fred Fox got her out of the cool green sanctuary and went in himself. It was dark. He groped around on the cool green carpet. He didn't know what he was looking for, but he found it, a small object lying in a far corner. He put it in his pocket and came out of the cloakroom.

'What'd you find, shamus?' asked Ben Rat apprehensively.

'Exhibit A,' said Fred Fox casually.

'Sahng plang keeng,' moaned Franz Frog.

'He says somebody's playing for keeps,' said Ben Rat.

'He can say that again,' said Fred Fox as the front door was flung open and Inspector Mastiff trotted in, followed by Sergeant Dachshund.

'Well, well, look who's muzzling in,' said Fred Fox.

'What have we got here?' barked Inspector Mastiff.

'I hate a private nose,' said Sergeant Dachshund.

Fred Fox grinned at him. 'What happened to your legs from the knees down, sport?' he asked.

'Drop dead,' snarled Sergeant Dachshund.

'Quiet, both of you!' snapped Inspector Mastiff. 'I know Ollie Owl, but who's the twenty-dollar Easter present from Schrafft's?' He turned on Fred Fox. 'If this bunny's head comes off and she's filled with candy, I'll have your badge, Fox,' he growled.

'She's real, Inspector,' said Fred Fox. 'Real dead, too. How did you pick up the scent?'

Inspector Mastiff howled. 'The Sergeant thought he smelt a rat at the Lily Club,' he said. 'Wrong again, as usual. Who's this dead rabbit?'

'She's my great-great-great-great-great-granddaughter,' sobbed old Mrs Rabbit.

Fred Fox lighted a cigarette. 'Oh, no, she isn't, sweetheart,' he said coolly. 'You are *her* great-great-great-great-great-granddaughter.' Pink lightning flared in the live white rabbit's eyes. 'You killed the old lady, so you could take over her carrot farm,' continued Fred Fox, 'and then you killed Hoot Owl.'

'I'll kill you, too, shamus!' shrieked Daphne Rabbit.

'Put the cuffs on her, Sergeant,' barked Inspector Mastiff. Sergeant Dachshund put a pair of handcuffs on the front legs of the dead rabbit. 'Not *her*, you dumb kraut!' yelped Inspector Mastiff. It was too late. Daphne Rabbit had jumped through a window-pane and run away, with the Sergeant in hot pursuit.

'All white rabbits look alike to me,' growled Inspector Mastiff. 'How could you tell them apart—from their ears?'

'No,' said Fred Fox. 'From their years. The white rabbit that called on me darn near beat me to the Lily Pad, and no old woman can do that.'

'Don't brag,' said Inspector Mastiff. 'Spryness isn't enough. What else?'

'She understood expressions an old rabbit doesn't know,' said Fred Fox, 'like "hop the hutch" and "throb" and "skip it" and "sap".'

'You can't hang a rabbit for her vocabulary,' said Inspector Mastiff. 'Come again.'

Fred Fox pulled the snapshot out of his pocket. 'The white rabbit who called on me told me Daphne was eighteen months old,' he said, 'but read what it says on the back of this picture.'

Inspector Mastiff took the snapshot, turned it over, and read, '"Daphne on her second birthday".'

'Yes,' said Fred Fox. 'Daphne knocked six months off her age. You see, Inspector, she couldn't read the writing on the snapshot, because those weren't her spectacles she was wearing.'

'Now wait a minute,' growled Inspector Mastiff. 'Why did she kill Hoot Owl?'

'Elementary, my dear Mastiff,' said Fred Fox. 'Hoot Owl lived in an oak tree, and she was afraid he saw her burrowing into the club last night, dragging Grandma. She heard Hoot Owl say, "I'm wise, I know everything," and so she killed him.'

'What with?' demanded the Inspector.

'Her right hind foot,' said Fred Fox. 'I was looking for a concealed weapon, and all the time she was carrying her heavy blunt instrument openly.'

'Well, what do you know!' exclaimed Inspector Mastiff. 'Do you think Hoot Owl really saw her?'

'Could be,' said Fred Fox. 'I happen to think he was bragging about his wisdom in general and not about a particular piece of information, but your guess is as good as mine.'

'What did you pick up in the cloakroom?' squeaked Ben Rat.

'The final strand in the rope that will hang Daphne,' said Fred Fox. 'I knew she didn't go in there to hide. She went in there to look for something she lost last night. If she'd been frightened, she would have hidden when the flies went out, but she went in there after the flies lighted up again.'

'That adds up,' said Inspector Mastiff grudgingly. 'What was it she was looking for?'

'Well,' said Fred Fox, 'she heard something drop in the dark when she dragged Grandma in there last night and she thought it was a button, or a buckle, or a bead, or a bangle, or a brooch that would incriminate her. That's why she rang me in on the case. She couldn't come here alone to look for it.'

'Well, what was it, Fox?' snapped Inspector Mastiff.

'A carrot,' said Fred Fox, and he took it out of his pocket, 'probably fell out of old Mrs Rabbit's reticule, if you like irony.'

'One more question,' said Inspector Mastiff. 'Why plant the body in the Lily Pad?'

'Easy,' said Fred Fox. 'She wanted to throw suspicion on the Croaker, a well-known lady-killer.'

'Nawng,' rumbled Franz Frog.

'Well, there it is, Inspector,' said Fred Fox, 'all wrapped up for you and tied with ribbons.'

Ben Rat disappeared into a wall. Franz Frog hopped back to his office.

'Mercy!' cried Sherman Stork. 'I'm late for an appointment!' He flew to the front door and opened it.

There stood Daphne Rabbit, holding the unconscious form of Sergeant Dachshund. 'I give up,' she said. 'I surrender.'

'Is he dead?' asked Inspector Mastiff hopefully.

'No,' said Daphne Rabbit. 'He fainted.'

'I never have any luck,' growled Inspector Mastiff.

Fred Fox leaned over and pointed to Daphne's right hind foot. 'Owl feathers,' he said. 'She's all yours, Inspector.'

'Thanks, Fox,' said Inspector Mastiff. 'I'll throw something your way someday.'

'Make it a nice, plump Plymouth Rocket pullet,' said Fred Fox, and he sauntered out of the Lily Pad.

JAMES THURBER: *Vintage Thurber*

Discuss what you know about the behaviour of lions, hyenas and jackals.

In fables and folk tales the lion often appears as the king of the beasts, i.e. a top person. In the first story, it says the lion was fair by nature. Does his behaviour strike you as fair?

Do you think the story was written by an underdog or a top dog?

Who is the laugh against?

Many fables end with a moral. Write a sentence giving a moral for this fable.

Write a fable of your own. The characters can be animals or machines or objects of any sort. End it with a moral.

Write a story, funny if possible, which shows a top person in a disreputable light (like the lion in the fable).

Discuss some of the jokes in The White Rabbit Caper.

Make a list of the various characters and the parts they play
e.g. Fred Fox: *private detective*.
Ben Rat: *doorman at the night club.*

Write out very briefly the plot of the story and how the mystery was solved.

Is it at all like any other crime or detective stories you have read?

Who is laughing at whom in this story?

See if you can write a story which 'takes the mickey' out of a popular kind, such as a Science fiction story, or a buried treasure story, a love story, a school story or even a fairy tale.

NO BOUNDARIES

11. Air and Water

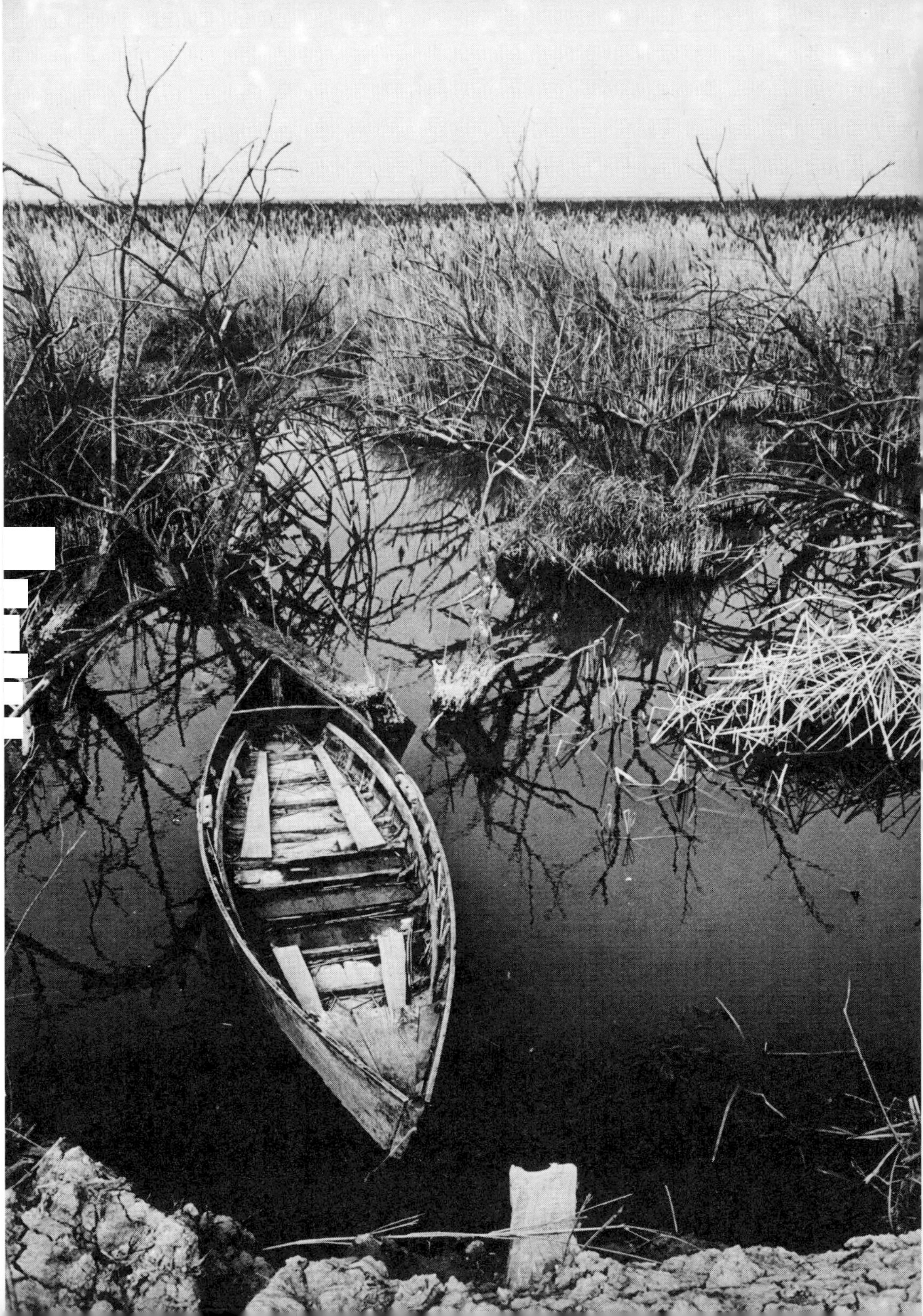

Flying the Kite

The soft and distant touch of the breeze as he reached the open piece of dirt set a longing feeling going inside him. He didn't know what it was he longed for, except that it was something that seemed to be beyond the paved street and houses and factories. . . .

'Howgo Michael!'

He turned and saw Herbert Duckworth carrying a kite. It was another high blue kite, and it looked like the tall sail of a ship up above Herbert. He seems to have shrunk since he started work in the mill.

'Howdo, Herbert', he said warmly. 'Ee, what a beauty!'

'She aren't too bad', said Herbert, raising it aloft. Under his arm he lugged an enormous reel of factory banding.

'I've had the paper ordered a week—it only came in today'.

'Where are you takin' her to get her up, Herbert?'

Herbert looked up at the Wild Goose chimney. 'There might be just enough wind to get her up from The Dirt', he said, watching the smoke roll quietly away into the distant sky.

'It won't give you much runnin' space, Herbert', he said.

'If I get a nice puff o' wind', said Herbert, 'she'll rise. Like to toss her for me Michael?'

'Yes, Herbert'.

He took the kite nervously.

'Hold a tick', said Herbert, 'whilst I check the tailin' '.

Herbert stretched the long tail out on the pavement, tightening the screws of paper along it. Then he took a big red dinner hanky from his pocket and tied it to the end of the tail. 'I fancy she'll do, Michael. Walk back as far as Wright's midden, an' I'll give thee a wave of my hand when I want her up'.

He walked along, bearing the big blue kite, shimmering and sighing in his hands. At the midden he turned and held it at the base of the standard, whilst Herbert pulled the string fairly taut. It's going to be a tricky toss-up. I hope I don't make a mess of it. They stood facing each other at a distance of a hundred yards. My arm's aching. Is there never going to be a breeze? Suddenly Herbert raised his hand and called: 'Right'.

He pushed the kite forcefully into the air just as the string went tight. The kite rose with a swish, as though an outpouring of breath left its body. It rose swiftly with the breeze and Herbert's quick dash. It went high above the housetops at one go, and then it gave a wild swing to the left, and looked as though it would duck downwards and smash itself on the pavement. He expected to see Herbert relax the tension and allow the kite to sink to the ground, but instead he gave it the breeze, and made it swing as much as it could, until it had either to rise or be smashed. The kite gave a squirm and rose. It went up higher and faster.

'Good lad, Herbert!' he called, running to him.

'Her's pullin' a bit to the left', said Herbert critically, 'but her's big enough an' her'll have to take it. I can't bring her in now. Her's a shade light in the tailin' too, but her'll steady once her gets up there.' His blue eyes had become light and large. . . .

Michael looked up along the curved string. Herbert said: 'Can tha' see it?'

'Aye, but only just', he said. The massive reel of white factory string was now down to an inch thickness.

'Still letting out, Herbert?' he asked.

'Aye, Michael', he said, 'she's got to go out of sight'.

He stood beside Herbert and watched. 'She's out of sight', he said. 'I can't see a speck of her'.

'We'll just give her an extra yard', said Herbert, and then he held the stick.

There was the reel of string, wound skilfully on a heavy round stick, held in Herbert's thin hands, and from it the string ran in a curve, up over Back Greenley street, over Holt's factory, and then right beyond all factories and chimneys, away out of sight in the distant evening sky.

'Herbert! Herbert!' One of his sisters was calling from the door-step.

'I've got to go to the outdoor licence for my dad's allowance', said Herbert. 'Michael, would tha' hold on till I come back?'

'Hold the kite, Herbert?'

'Aye, she'll be all right. Steady as an eagle, but pullin'. Just hold on an' I'll be back in five minutes'.

He took the stick of string from Herbert and held it. It was a strange sensation to feel the pull of the kite. He looked along the string that went up into the sky and disappeared. It's like there was someone up there pullin' at you from another world. . . . He felt someone coming near him and he half turned.

'How's she been pullin', Michael?' asked Herbert, taking over the kite and giving the string a few tugs.

'Strong', he said. 'Her's been pullin' strong. Can tha' feel them flecks o' rain, Herbert?'

'Aye, I thought I did feel a drop then.'

'Tha'd better pull in then, eh?'

Herbert looked at the winding-on stick. 'I don't like havin' a kite up', he said, 'without goin' bare stick'.

'You're not lettin' more off, Herbert?' he asked.

Already Herbert was giving the kite more string.

'Aye,' he said, 'I don't reckon to let my kite up without I give it all the bandin' I've got. It's half-hearted, and watch it tak' it!' The string was moving swiftly through his hand. Every few seconds he stopped and gave a feeling tug at the kite string. The kite itself was completely out of sight. He stared at Herbert: what faith made him send his great kite even farther into the unknown sky? 'Only a few more yards', said Herbert, 'bare stick an' then wind in.'

He looked down at the almost emptied stick jiggling on the ground, when suddenly he saw the end of string leave the stick and rise. 'The string—grab it' he screamed.

Herbert made a snatch at the departing string but just missed. They both darted after it as it was pulled swiftly along the pavement, stamping on it with their clogs. They missed it, and ran to the wall of Back Greenley Street, and Herbert struck with his flat hand against the wall to imprison the moving wisp of string. For one moment he held it but then it pulled

itself free. He made a grab after Herbert as he saw it rise up the side of the house. It was too late. The string went over the house and disappeared. It'll be falling, falling, falling far, far away. Falling like a great broken bird, far from the street. Herbert's face was strained and grey.

'Well, that's the last I'll ever see o' that, Michael'.

'Eee, I'm sorry, Herbert' he said, 'I saw it come up an' I shouted'.

'I'll never understand how that string weren't tied on to the windin'-on-stick', said Herbert. 'I've never known it. It's the first thing I do—tie it on. I must have forgot'. He went back and picked up the smooth black stick. 'Here, Michael', he said, 'that's a good windin'-on stick. Thee have it'.

'Ta, Herbert'.

Herbert looked once more upward to the faraway empty evening sky. 'I wonder' he said calmly, 'where she fell?'

'Oh, o'er the Pennine Chain, Herbert' he said. 'Aye, I'll bet, an' beyond'.

'Her pulled a bit to the left', Herbert said, 'but I wouldn't ha' altered her'.

They looked up the street and saw the lads coming down after their walk. The chairs had all gone in and no one had noticed the incident.

From *One Small Boy* by BILL NAUGHTON

This passage about flying a kite is taken from a story about an Irish boy growing up in a Northern industrial town. He describes exactly how they launched the kite and how they lost it. He also writes what the boys said to each other, so there is conversation and action here, but there is more than this. The boys don't actually say all that they feel about the kite. Michael is anxious most of the time; Herbert is very confident and very proud and fond of his kite. They both feel there is something special about sending the big kite up out of sight and still controlling it themselves from the ground. They do not speak about these feelings directly, but from time to time we hear a third 'voice' in the story; this is the writer speaking, telling his readers something which the 'characters' didn't say, and perhaps don't know, but which the writer knows and wants his readers to know.

Write a story about making or playing with or using something that was precious to you. Try to describe exactly what you did, include some conversation and see if you can also say something about how you and your companions felt and thought, and this will be the extra voice—the voice of you, as a writer. Some of you will be more familiar with making and launching model gliders than with kites; others will have launched and sailed model boats; others will have built sand-castles and fortifications against an incoming tide, or damned up streams, or built houses in trees, or made puppets, or baked a cake.

The Boy and the River

All this happened a very long time ago, and I am now almost an old man. But no matter how long my life may last, I shall never forget those days of my boyhood which I spent on the river. They were lovely, and I can still live them over again. Their freshness is in no way dimmed. What I saw then I can see again today. I have only to give rein to my thoughts to become once more the lad whose waking eyes were enchanted by the world of waters which he had just discovered.

When I awoke dawn was just breaking. The first thing I saw was the sky, nothing but the sky. It was grey and mauve. Very high up, on a thread of cloud, but nowhere else, there was a faint flush of pink. . . . Some bird or other—it may have been a warbler—was uttering its call. . . . Then the clumps of reed were swept by a flutter of wet wings, and, all about the boat, the confused murmur of water-creatures rose into the air; . . . I listened. . . . The boat lay without movement. . . .

My companion was still asleep. He lay at full length on his back with his face turned to the sky. Sleep had struck his features to utter stillness. They were brown and sinewy, and his cheek-bones stood out prominently. The nose was short with small and rounded nostrils. The lips looked as though they were clenched on sleep with a fury of concentration. Two black lashed lids covered the closed eyes. The mask of sleep was an outer and visible symbol of the wild young life within. . . .

When the sun, passing over the reeds, touched him, his eyes opened at once.

He saw me and smiled. The hard expression of the serious young face relaxed suddenly, and its place was taken by a smile so sweet that it completely bowled me over.

'Pascalet', murmured Gatzo . . .

I smiled back. We were friends.

It was then that the time of the sleeping waters began. We lived for ten days hidden in a back-water which led nowhere. . . .

This backwater was on the left bank of the river (that is to say, on the side opposite to the one on which I was born) and drove deep into a low, flat countryside. We were separated from the main bank by an inextricable tangle of water plants which afforded complete concealment. Along the bank itself stood a thick wall of alders. Closer to us were bushes of guelder-rose, patches of gorse, and vast expanses of protective reeds. These were of every variety: marsh reeds, bulrushes, passion-reeds, and reeds of the scented kind. From the virgin mud they rose into the air tough and long-lived. Here and there among the blue-green waters they formed impenetrable islets.

Our backwater eventually lost itself in a confusion of innumerable water-ways. Some of these flowed across the vegetable archipelago, and gradually disappeared under a leafy roof. Others penetrated deep into the land, shaded by lines of willows. All were objects of mystery. Their waters slept beneath the sun, though here and there the invisible current carried along little scraps of arrow-headed blossom and bog-myrtle.

These sights enchanted me. Gatzo, on the contrary, seemed to be indifferent to them. He did not talk much. . . . But we understood one another, for I, too, have a love of silence. But if I said nothing it was for the pleasure of saying nothing. . . . My thinking was of the lazy kind, a loitering, wandering, vagabond thinking, that half-awake movement of the mind which is the chosen hunting-ground of useless day-dreams. . . .

'You're like a sleep-walker!' Gatzo would say to me, irritably.

For him there was a sharp, harsh line of division between sleep and wakefulness.

'When I sleep', he said, 'I do what is necessary. I shut my eyes and think of nothing. That rests me. When you sleep you turn and twist and mutter, and that spoils your rest . . . .'

To this I made no reply. He was perfectly right, but I felt hurt.

That first day of ours in the backwater was wonderful. I have never known one to hold a candle to it. I think of it as the loveliest of my life. We began it by making a thorough examination of our craft, and were rewarded by the discovery of many treasures. There were two lockers chock-full of odds and ends. One of these was for'ard, and contained fishing tackle of every description: gut, floats, hooks, lines, lobster-pots, drag-nets, ledger-lines. The other one, aft, was stuffed with provisions, all in tins, so that we had nothing to fear from moisture . . . .

This particular find delighted us. There was coffee and sugar, a keg of flour, dried vegetables, spices, a bottle of oil, and—oh, all sorts of things . . . enough, certainly to keep us going for a week.

The boat itself was equipped with two pairs of oars.

The hull was in good shape and appeared to be thoroughly watertight. The paint was sound. A brass compass had been fixed for'ard on the deck. To us it was an object of wonder, for it showed thirty-two points, and carried the names of sixteen winds, each lovelier than the last: Labe, Gregali, Tramontane . . . .

'We must keep it well shined', said Gatzo excitedly: 'it's our mascot'.

We gave the whole of our attention to polishing it until it shone.

Round the compass-card the name of the ship to which it belonged was written in gold letters: 'La Mourette'.

'They stole it', said Gatzo: 'and I know where too, but it's a long way from here'.

He pointed upstream.

Far away, scarcely visible, was a blue smudge of hills.

'There?' I asked.

'There', he answered: 'a jolly bit of country'.

What country? From where had Gatzo journeyed to the island? Who was he?

I asked myself these questions, but never dared to put them to him. My presence on the island, my unexpected appearance must have puzzled him. But he showed no curiosity about these miraculous happenings which only I seemed to find wonderful.

For there were moments when I told myself that I was living in a dream, a terrifying yet delicious dream . . . .

How, if it were not a dream, could I have found myself, after so many adventures alone with a boy whose name was the only thing I knew of him, and on this boat, this hidden boat, lost from human sight among the reeds up a backwater which led nowhere?

From *The Boy and the River* by HENRI BOSCO

This incident is taken from a story by a French writer about a great river in the south of France where it is very hot in summer. He tells you about the river, about the two boys and how different they were, about the boat and the mysteriousness of the whole adventure.

Here are some suggestions for your own writing.

A story about a river which you explored with one companion on foot or in a boat. It can be any sort of a river; a very big one like this coming from distant hills and spreading out into innumerable waterways which get smaller and smaller until they are just reed beds; or a small stream running between trees with clear shallow pools. Such a story ought to have a map or a picture map to go with it.

Being in a boat; on the sea, or a lake, a river or even a pond; write what you saw around you, what you did, how you felt. A poem might do this best.

Write a continuation of the adventures of Pascalet and Gatzo. This passage describes their first day in their boat on the backwater of the great river; what do you think they did next? There were many things to do; fish to be caught and cooked; a fire to be made somehow; there must have been people living near the river so they must have come to a village sometime; perhaps they bought fresh bread to eat with their fish and tinned provisions; what did they do for water to drink?

If you know part of a river well, write about the things you know about it which a casual visitor would not notice.

12. Bedtime

As we lie in bed on the edge of falling asleep we relax; we stop being watchful or curious, or energetic; things from this day, or other days slip through our minds; we half dream and sleepily hear the familiar sounds of the household going on as from a distance, and feel safe and warm; though it is also a time when fears can easily rise and if we wake suddenly in the night we feel strange and alarmed until we remember where we are and can identify whatever has waked us.

For a long time I used to go to bed early. Sometimes, when I had put out my candle, my eyes would close so quickly that I had not even time to say 'I'm going to sleep'. And half an hour later the thought that it was time to go to sleep would awaken me; I would try to put away the book which, I imagined, was still in my hands, and to blow out the light. . . . I would ask myself what o'clock it could be; I could hear the whistling of trains, which, now nearer, and now farther off, punctuating the distance like the note of a bird in a forest, showed me the deserted countryside through which a traveller would be hurrying towards the nearest station . . . I would lay my cheeks gently against the comfortable cheeks of my pillow . . . and revisit in the long course of my waking dream, my room in winter, where on going to bed I would at once bury my head in a nest, built up out of the most diverse materials, the corner of my pillow, the top of my blankets, a piece of shawl, the edge of my bed, and a copy of an evening paper, all of which things I would contrive, with the infinite patience of birds building their nests, to cement into one whole; a room where, in a keen frost, I would feel the satisfaction of being shut in from the outer world (like the sea-swallow which builds at the end of a dark tunnel and is kept warm by the surrounding earth), and where, the fire keeping in all night, I would sleep wrapped up, as it were, in a great cloak of snug and savoury air, shot with the glow of the logs which would break out again in flame: in a sort of alcove without walls, a cave of warmth dug out of the heart of the room itself, a zone of heat whose boundaries were constantly shifting and altering in temperature as gusts of air ran across them to strike freshly upon my face, from the corners of the room, or from parts near the window or far from the fireplace which had therefore remained cold.

From *Swann's Way* by MARCEL PROUST

Boating

Gently the river bore us
   Beneath the morning sky,
Singing, singing, singing
Its reedy quiet tune
   As we went floating by;
And all the afternoon
   In our small boat we lay
Rocking, rocking, rocking
   Under the willows grey
When into bed that evening
   I climbed, it seemed a boat
Was softly rocking, rocking,
Rocking me to sleep,
   And I was still afloat
I heard the grey leaves weep
   And whisper round my bed,
The river singing, singing,
   Singing through my head.

From *The Blackbird in the Lilac* by JAMES REEVES

A Bedtime Story

Owls hoot outside my window,
My dog barks from down stairs,
But I am in bed, tucked up,
         Safe and warm,
While my mother and father
         Talk in the kitchen.

BEDTIME

A clatter of feet on our garden path,
A slam of a wooden gate,
Announces, my big brother Charlie,
Has come home again, very late.

RICHARD aged 11

Rain

I woke in the swimming dark
And heard, now sweet, now shrill,
The voice of the rain-water,
    Cold and still,

Endlessly sing; now faint,
In the distance borne away;
Now in the air float near,
    But nowhere stay;

Singing I know not what,
Echoing on and on;
Following me in sleep,
    Till night was gone.

WALTER DE LA MARE

Here are some suggestions for your writing.

A poem (or a piece of prose) called 'Bedtime' about your feelings and thoughts when you are lying in bed on the edge of falling asleep.

A dream you have had more than once.

A poem about the things you see when you shut your eyes.

A story about a boy or girl who was afraid of the dark.

APPENDIX 1

How to Correct Your Own Written Work

Printers' and Authors' Symbols for Correcting Proofs. Adapted from the British Standards Institution.

All your main corrections should be made in the margin, but you will also need to mark the place in the text where the correction has to be made.

This is what you have to do when you are correcting a manuscript, or a story in an exercise book.

When you notice a mistake you put a mark in the margin. The *left*-hand column below tells you which particular mark to make, and the *centre* column tells you what it means. But you must also show the writer (or the printer) exactly which bit of the writing you want altered, so as well as the mark in the margin, you also mark the text. The *right*-hand column tells you how to mark the text. For example, if a capital letter is needed instead of a small letter, you should write "caps" in the margin and put three strokes under the small letter that you want altered in the text. An example of a corrected story by a boy of eleven is given after the table.

There are some technical words you will need to know for accurate correcting.

Text: What is written, typed or printed.
Insert: Put in.
Substitute: Put instead of.
Delete: Take out.
Table: Diagram with information in columns and rows.

	Marginal mark	Meaning	Corresponding mark in text
1	₰	Delete (take out)	/
2	caps	Change to capital letters	≡ under letters or words to be altered.

	Marginal mark	Meaning	Corresponding mark in text
3	*underline*	Underline word or words	——— under words affected
4	#	Space between lines or paragraphs	>
5	*n.p.*	Begin a new paragraph	[before first word of new paragraph
6	*run on*	No fresh paragraph here	⊃ between paragraphs
7	*spell out*	The abbreviation or figure to be spelt out in full	encircle words or figures to be altered
8	⅄	Something left out: insert matter indicated in margin	⅄
9	,⅄	Insert comma	⅄
10	,/	Substitute comma	/
11	⊙⅄	Insert full-stop	⅄
12	⊙/	Substitute full-stop	/
13	?⅄	Insert question mark	⅄
14	?/	Substitute question mark	/
15	!⅄	Insert exclamation mark	⅄
16	’⅄	Insert apostrophe	⅄
17	”⅄	Insert quotation marks	⅄
18	(?)	I don't understand this	encircle words, etc. affected

Here is an example of how a manuscript is corrected for printing according to the table above. This piece is about budgerigars and is by a boy of eleven.

The proof reader's corrections have been numbered so that they may be discussed. Every proof-reader would correct number 1, 3, 5, 6, 7, 8, 10, and 11 in exactly this way; but numbers 2, 4, 9, and 12 would get different treatment from different people, so they need to be discussed.

The moral of this is that even printers and teachers do not always agree, so you need to know what you are doing yourself.

Use the proof-correction sheet to correct a piece written by someone else in your class.

If you do this from time to time you will find it easier to revise your own work.

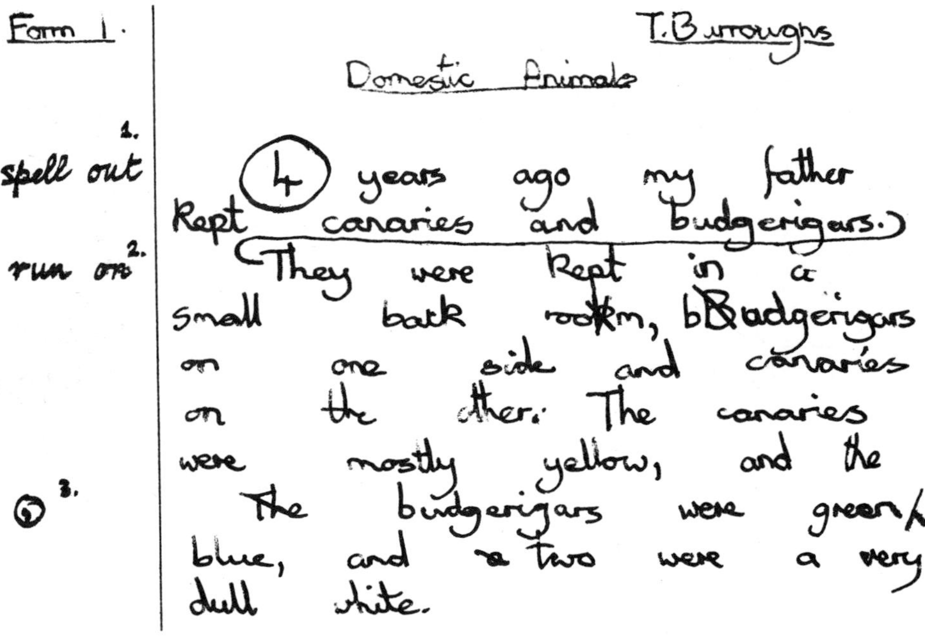

Form 1. T. Burroughs

Domestic Animals

1. spell out — 4 years ago my father
kept canaries and budgerigars.
2. run on — They were kept in a
small back room, budgerigars
on one side and canaries
on the other. The canaries
were mostly yellow, and the
3. — The budgerigars were green/
blue, and two were a very
dull white.

One day my father found
that a canary was dead.
run on[4] It was breeding time and
there was ^ one egg left whole,
with ^three or four others
smashed on the floor, and in
the cage. The next night
my father hid in the
back room with his torch.
The next morning he
told us that he had seen
a rat ^like creature and
^ o [5] frightened it off. It was to^
big for a mouse and a
bit small for a rat.
About nine months ago
we had a nice white
budgeirgar called Snowy. One
^ o [6] day he wasn't feeling to^
good so I took him to a
vet. A few days later we
(ei) [7] recieved a letter saying that
the fumes from the oil heater
(were) [8] ~~was~~ harming him, so he
should be kept away from

O

9. it/ He was kept in the same room as the other budgerigars and one day a
10. whistling tune came on the wireless. Snowy was very fond of these songs and this one he did not sing to.
I went into the room he was in where I found him lying in the strange
11. were position. There ~~was~~ no marks
12. cap/ on him/ then a nearby neighbour told us of his bird dying with fright. He then told us of a strange rat like creature which he saw a few nights before.

We never found out about this but now my father has grown fond of dogs.

APPENDIX 2

Spelling

If you had grown up to speak Welsh instead of English you would not have had nearly so much difficulty with spelling because the Welsh language is still spelt very much as it is pronounced. A good guess according to how the words sound would be right as often as not, but English children are not so lucky. Spelling according to how the words sound may produce something like the following which is from the last chapter of a novel by a girl of nine. She wrote it about 1900 and it is called *The Young Visiters* by Daisy Ashford.

Mr Salteena by the aid of the earl and the kindness of the Prince of Wales managed to get the job his soul craved and any day might be seen in Hyde Park or Pickadilly gallopping madly after the Royal Carrage in a smart suit of green velvit with knicker boccers compleat. At first he was rarther terrifide as he was not used to riding and he found his horse bumped him a good deal and he had to cling on desperatly to its flowing main. At other times the horse would stop dead and Mr Salteena would use his spurs and bad languige with no avail.

How many spelling mistakes can you find?

There is nothing much we can do about the difficulty of English spelling except learn it, but learning to spell can be made easier in several ways.

Here are some ways in which, over a year or so, you can improve your spelling considerably.

1. Use a dictionary.

If you are a very bad speller you may not find a dictionary very helpful at first. You have to have some idea how a word is spelt before you can find it in a dictionary, but the better you become at spelling the more useful you will find it.

2. Do as much proof-correcting of other people's compositions as you can. By correcting other people's work and checking their spelling with a dictionary you should improve your own.

3. Read Appendix 3 so that you understand *why* English spelling does not usually represent the sounds, and be on the look out for groups of words which are spelt in the same way.

4. Make your own word book. Collect and enter words under headings that interest you. Some you might use are: New Words, Odd Words, Foreign Words, Words I cannot usually spell, Trap Words, and so on. Learn them and try them out on your friends, particularly grown-ups.

5. Four spelling rules. There are so many exceptions to the rules of English spelling that they can't really be called rules, but here are four of the commonest ones which you may find helpful, though the best way of learning to spell is to read a lot and notice the words. People who read a lot are usually quite good spellers. They pick it up in passing.

(a) Silent e and -i-n-g. Words like fade, ride, hope, stoke, make, bake, line, hate, love, exercise, educate, estimate, etc., drop their final e when you turn them into -ing words such as fading, riding, hoping, hating, loving, exercising, educating, etc.

(b) Full and -ful. When you add full to another word you leave off one of the l's. For example, help—helpful, beauty—beautiful, truth—truthful, shame—shameful, etc.

(c) Donkeys and ponies and ladies. If a word ends in y in the singular, you change the y into -ies when you write about more than one. For example, pony—ponies, lady—ladies, beauty—beauties, gipsy—gipsies, mummy—mummies, silly—sillies, etc.

But if it ends in -ey like donkey, you just add s. For example donkey—donkeys,

(d) Girl's hat, boy's bat. You show ownership by adding 's' to the name of the owner. A girl's hat, a boy's bat, Jane's hair, Peter's penkife, Alice's umbrella, Mary's Mother, a flower's scent, a man's money, etc.

BUT when there are two or more owners you just add apostrophe. For example, girls' hats, boys' bats, donkeys' ears, ponies' tails, gipsies' tents, Heroes' medals, etc.

6. **Words have a shape**, and groups of words have similar shapes. One of the ways of learning to spell words is to let your hand help your eye and your memory by writing the words down. The fingers of trained typists do much of their owners' spelling for them. Another way of helping yourself to spell is to look at a word that you want to learn, such as 'assistant' or 'changeable', then shut your eyes and try to see it in print in your mind's eye.

7. **Be bold about words**! It is much better to use new words even if you misspell them, than to play safe and only use the words that you know how to spell.

APPENDIX 3

Why English spelling is difficult

Words, like everything else, change. They change their look, that is their spelling, and they change their meaning. Here are a few lines of English as it was written in the time of Ethelred the Unready. This kind of English is called Old English (O.E. in the dictionary).

The Danes come to Devon

Her com se here to Exanmuthan, ond up tha eadon to thaere byrig ond thaer faestlice waeron; ac him man swythe heardlice withstod tha wendon he geonod thaet land, ond dydon eall swa he bewune waeron; slogon ond baerndon.

From *The Anglo-Saxon Chronicles* for the year 1001

This means roughly: In this year the raiding army came to Exmouth and then inland to the fort and there they attacked persistently, but the defenders valiantly withstood them. Then they scattered throughout that land and did everything they were accustomed to do, slaying and burning.

England was conquered by the Normans in 1066 and for 300 years two languages were spoken, French by the nobles and merchants and English by the peasants. Of course, most people spoke a little of the other language too, but because it was a foreign language for them, they often got much of it wrong and gradually the more difficult parts of the English language were lost because the Normans could not use it correctly. At the same time the English came to use many words and expressions which they learned from their French masters, so by about 1350 English had changed a great deal. It looked and sounded rather like French. Here are a few lines from Chaucer who wrote this about 1390.

Here begynneth the Man of Lawe his Tale.

In Surrye whilom swelte a companye
Of chapmen riche, and therto sadde and trewe,
That wyde where senten hir spicerye,
Cloths of gold, and satins riche of hewe;
Hir chaffare was so thrifty and so newe,
That every wight hath deyntee to chaffare
With hem, and eek ito sellen hem hir ware.

'The Man of Lawe's Tale' from *The Canterbury Tales* by GEOFFREY CHAUCER

This means roughly: In Syria at one time dwelt a company of merchants, rich, sober and honest, who sent their goods everywhere abroad—spices and cloth made of gold and different coloured satin. Their dealing was so good that everyone wanted to buy from them and also to sell to them.

This form of our language is called Middle English (M.E. in the dictionary).

Printing was not brought to England till 1475 and up to this time all the 'books' were written by hand, mostly by the monks on parchment (very thin, smooth skin). As the monks were nearly all educated in France, and French was the official language of England until 1352, their attempts to spell English names (and other words when they had to use them) were rather like your attempts to spell in French would be. They spelt words as they sounded to them, and since very different kinds of English were spoken in the North of England, the Midlands, Sussex, and Somerset, there were dozens of different spellings of the same words, and no one thought that the writers were uneducated because of this, as would be the case today.

In 1475 Caxton set up his printing press in Westminster and produced the first English printed book. It was a book for children on good manners. His third book was called *Le Morte D'Arthur* by Sir Thomas Malory ('The Death of Arthur') and was a collection of well-known and very popular stories about the Knights of the Round Table. Caxton had spent thirty years in Germany and Holland learning about printing and he brought over Dutch printers to help him set up the type and print his books. They, like the monks, spelt words as they heard them, but English to a Dutchman would sound different from the way it sounded to French monks so here again was a cause of yet more different spellings of the same words.

The result of printing was that instead of there being perhaps half a dozen hand-writen copies of a manuscript in England, there could now be several hundred printed copies of every book. And, of course, many more different books were printed. It is easier for a printer who is setting up type to spell the same word the same way every time he puts the type together, so gradually the printers' way of spelling words became more widely used; some 300 years after Caxton many words had come to be spelt in the same way, and well-educated people used the same spellings.

In 1755 the first dictionary was published. It was compiled by Dr. Samuel Johnson who loved books, cats, tea, and talking to people. As it was the first, and only dictionary at that time, writers and educated people and printers all consulted his dictionary when they were doubtful how to spell words. Since then our spelling hasn't changed much, but our pronunciation has, so there is now a big gap between the way we say words and the way they are spelt.

The Americans have changed their spelling a little to make it more like speech, for example 'Honor' instead of 'Honour' and 'Thru' instead of 'Through'; and on advertisements and shop signs many words are spelt as they sound. But in printed books and newspapers American spelling is still only slightly different from English spellings.

One way of learning to spell is to do your own proof-correcting. To do this you will need a dictionary, a proof-correcting sheet giving the signs (see page 206 Appendix 1) and quite a lot of practice on your own or other people's manuscripts (compositions).

APPENDIX 4

Arranging a Programme

1. *Get into a workable size group (six to eight people).*
2. *Appoint someone to write things down.*
3. *Choose a chairman or group leader who will help you keep yourselves in order.*
4. *Find out what talent you have in the group; good speakers, good readers, people who can sing, or work a tape-recorder.*

Suggested length of programme for the group: 10–15 minutes.

Suggestions for Programmes

1. *Poems and music on a theme. Your own poems and poems from books.*
   Sleep.
   Animals.
   Indoors and out.
   Comfort and fear.
   Laughter and tears.
   Loneliness and company.
2. *A ballad programme. Sung if possible.*
   Heroes and villains.
   Escape.
   Ghosts and apparitions.

'The course of true love never did run smooth.'
Ships and sailors.
Sea shanties and work songs.
Songs of the underdog.
Revenge.

3. *Poems. Solo and in chorus.*
The sea and the seaside.
Mystery.
Rain and wind and sunshine.
Nonsense, jokes, and outrageous poems.
Home and away from home.

4. *Favourite Poems. Each member of the group chooses one.*

5. *Documentary or imaginary documentary. Reports, bits of newscasting, bits of conversation, mime, music, sound effects.*
Journey through space.
Guy Fawkes night.
Market.
The circus.
A procession.
A transformation: Cinderella becomes an elegant lady;
The frog becomes a prince;
Sleeping Beauty awakes;
A caterpillar becomes a pupa and then a butterfly;
Dick Whittington becomes Lord Mayor of London.

Choosing what is to go in

When you have decided on your theme, find poems that you like, and choose ones that are in different moods—sad, exciting, satiric for example. Avoid choosing pieces that are too much alike.

Music. Choose a record to play before, after or (very softly) during the poems. It should seem suitable to go with the poems.

When you have decided what you want to put in your programme, rehearse it several times. Try to join the music in smoothly.

Audience. Invite them! Another class your own age perhaps?

The performance

Get one member of the group to introduce the programme, saying clearly and fairly slowly what the theme is.

If you have made a tape of your programme, and are playing the tape instead of performing it 'live', try out the tape-recorder before you begin. Appoint one person to work it. The rest of the group should be out of sight, or in the audience.

If you are doing your programme 'live', the group should be as quiet as professional actors, except when they are reading or singing.

APPENDIX 5

Conversations and other voices

'What is the use of a book,' thought Alice, 'without pictures or conversation.'

Do you agree with Alice? Do you like conversation in stories or do you think it holds up the narrative?

In the story called 'A Visit to the Zoo' *there is only one voice: the boy who is telling the story. Who do you think he was talking to in his mind as he wrote?*

In 'The Dog with a Million Fleas' there are three characters, the boy who tells the story, his mother, and the stranger boy whom he meets in the wood. But the boy who is telling the story has two voices. One of them speaks aloud, and the other speaks in his mind, to himself as it were.

The things that are said aloud, the actual conversation, is marked in the story by quotation marks, for example, 'That's my dog. He's called Ruff.' All the rest is the writer telling what happened and what he thought and felt.

Quotation marks are a sign that a conversation has taken place and you are invited to listen to what was said as if you were there and could hear the actual voices. If you *report* what someone said yesterday, or an hour ago, or last week, or last year, you don't use quotation marks.

Look at the last two paragraphs of 'The Dog with a Million Fleas' *and see if you understand why in one case what Stuart's mother said is in quotation marks and in the other it is not.*

Quotation marks are not usually used in poems.

The writer of 'The Summer of the Beautiful White Horse' has chosen not to use quotation marks and there is a lot of conversation in this story. *Do you find any difficulty in following it?*

In this story every time a different person speaks, the writer starts a new line. This is another way of showing who is speaking.

So there are two ways of showing speech when you write a story.

(*a*) Put quotation marks round the words that represent the voice of the person speaking.

(*b*) Take a new line for each different speaker.

These 'rules' are like many other 'rules' of behaviour; they are the good manners of writing, designed to help the *reader*. They don't help the writer, except when he comes to read what he has written.

Can you think of any other 'rules' of writing which are designed to help the reader?

APPENDIX 6

The English of English and the English of other subjects

Overleaf is a page from a twelve year old boy's Geography exercise book. It is a write-up of his observations made during a Geography walk. His teacher gave it a good mark, yet it is very unlike most of the written work in his English book (which also gained good marks).

Study it carefully and then see if you can make any observations about the kind of English used. Here are some questions to help you.

1. *How would you read this? Top to bottom? Block by block? Left to right? Line by line?*
2. *Could you read it aloud so that a listener could understand it, or is it not meant to be read aloud?*

ROCKS AND SOILS IN THE HARROW AREA

	Appearance	Place	Trees & Plants	Use to Farmer
Pebble gravel	Dark Grey and very dry and very pebbly.	High ground i.e. Bushey Heath.	Thin spindly plants and trees i.e. Birch, Pine, bracken	None except making paths
London clay	Fine sticky soil. It is so fine no water can pass through	Lower slopes and valleys	Most common trees ash, Oak.	Cows and grass. ✓
Chalk	White, Powdery and very fine often found with flints	Hills.	very light grass and on the lower slopes Beech	none except now they can use it for pasture
Silt or Alluvium	Very dark and fine soil.	Low lying ground near rivers	Oak and other trees that thrive on damp soils	very fertile. good for cows and nearly all crops. Very good
				8/10

3. *What is it about?*
4. *Is it like or different from the English you would use in stories or conversation?*
5. *What can you say about the actual language (words and sentences)?*
6. *Why do you think the English of this set of observations is like this? What is it for?*

It would be quite possible to write up this information in another way. Try a first paragraph, using this information.

On a walk you notice (or ignore) all sorts of things. What you specially notice depends on what you are interested in—what your eyes pick out and focus on. This boy was focusing on a few particular things. No doubt he observed other things but he didn't write about them. Why not?

Write about a page in which you describe an expedition you went on with your class, but only put into it anything that interested you or that you remember vividly. Use the first person ('I' or 'We').

Read your piece through and notice what things interested you enough to get into your story. What were you focussing on? Objects, people, things that happened, your feelings, your teacher?

Do you reckon your piece is a good one? or don't you know until you get your book back and see your mark or comment?

Do you think all your school subjects have their own particular kinds of English? Would some of them go into groups according to the kind of English you use for them?

Try making a table for different kinds of English.

It might be something like this:

	Subject	Language	Useful or to please yourself
Notes	History Science	Bits of sentences. Special words	
Observations	Geography Biology		Either or both

continued next page

Accounts of things	History	Proper sentences. Special words. Paragraphs.	
Reports of experiments		Don't use 'I'	
Stories	History English	Can write about anything. Longer pieces. Can use 'I'	To please yourself (or your teacher?)
Poems			

Can you fill in the blank cells in this table?

Ted Hughes is a poet; he wrote *The Thought Fox* on p. 105. Here is what he has to say about writing a poem. Keep your eye on the ball is his advice—the ball being whatever it is you want to say.

. . . When the words are pouring out, how can you be sure that you don't have one of the side-meanings of the word 'feathers' getting all stuck up with one of the side-meanings of the word 'treacle', a few words later. In bad poetry this is exactly what happens, the words kill each other.

Luckily, you don't have to bother about it so long as you do one thing.

That one thing is, simply imagine what you're writing about. See it and live it. Don't think it up laboriously, as if you were working out mental arithmetic. Just look at it, touch it, smell it, listen to it, turn yourself into it. When you do this, the words look after themselves, like magic. If you do this, you don't have to bother about commas or full-stops or that sort of thing. You don't look at the words either, you keep your eyes, your ears, your nose, your taste, your touch, your whole being, on the thing you're turning into words. The minute you flinch, and take your mind off this thing, and begin to look at the words and worry about them, then your worry goes into them and they set about killing each other. So you keep going as long as you can, then look back and see what you've written.

After a bit of practice, and after telling yourself a few times that you don't care how other people have written about this thing, this is the way you find it; and after telling yourself you're going to use any old word that comes into your head so long as it seems right at the moment of writing it down, you'll surprise yourself. You'll read back through what you've written and you'll get a shock. You'll have captured a spirit, a creature.

From *Capturing Animals* by TED HUGHES

This advice would be equally good for many things that you write in English lessons.

APPENDIX 7

Ballads and folksongs

Towards the end of the 19th century changes in printing machines made it possible to produce newspapers by the million very quickly. After this people could read in the papers every day all the sensational things which nearly everyone at heart wants to hear about.

Before this, great deeds, bad deeds, acts of violence, and horror and grief and love and bravery got made into ballads and spread over the country because people like to sing, and to listen to singing. Many ballads and folksongs are very old; others are more recent. Up to the end of the 19th century you can find songs and ballads about most things that people did which involved struggle and violent feelings.

Here are some examples:

Robin Hood and his men. A popular hero who outwits the rich and powerful.

Border ballads about battles between Scottish and English Knights.

Ballads about battles and bravery, such as Agincourt, Flodden and the Spanish Armada.

Sad ballads about the loss of a ship, the death of a leader, or about hangings and beheadings.

Sad ballads about faithless lovers, and betrayals, and fearful crimes (e.g. Lammerlinkin on p. 120).

Ballads about ghosts and hauntings and revenge.

Ballads about the Press Gang, about whaling, about soldiers enlisting for a shilling a day, about highwaymen and beggars.

And ballads with mocking or nonsensical choruses about extraordinary and outrageous creatures.

There are also many American songs and ballads about gold-diggers, cowboys, frontiersmen, railroad men and hobos of all sorts. The Buffalo Skinners is an example of one of these (see p. 162).

You can find the words and the music of many ballads and folksongs in:

1. *The Penguin Book of Folksongs.*
2. *Folksongs of the U.S.A.* Ed. Alan Lomax.
3. Recordings of ballads sung by well known singers or by local people, such as:

   Shuttle and Cage: Industrial Folk Ballads, (Ewan MacColl);
   Sea Shanties, (Ewan MacColl);
   Diesel and Slate, (Cyril Tawney);
   Springhill Mining Disaster, (MacColl and Seeger);
   Danny Deever, (Bernard Miles);
   Border Ballads, (John Laurie);
   English and Scottish Popular Ballads, (Folkways Records FG 3509).

APPENDIX 7

Cecil Sharp House, 2 Regents Park Road, London N.W.1 is the centre for people interested in folksong, and folk-sings are held there frequently.

No one knows who made up the folk songs and ballads. There are many different versions of most of them and singers today feel quite free to leave out verses or alter some of the words if they want to. And this has probably been going on for a long time. People change them to suit the occasion. Because these songs have no particular author they are called folk songs: songs of the people.

Although they are not so common as they used to be, ballads and songs on subjects that a lot of people feel strongly about still get composed and sung. There are ballads for instance about mine disasters, and strikes and revolutionary political songs, and some modern poets write ballads. *The Griesly Wife* on p. 116 for instance is by a contemporary Australian writer.

Popular heroes have always been subject matter for ballads. Here is one written by a thirteen year old boy called Ron about a famous footballer. What do you think of it?

The Ballad of Hughie Gallagher

There was a little calliper-legged man,
Who always carried a chip on his shoulder
Because of only being five feet tall.

Hughie was what anyone could call him,
His movement was like grease lightning
And weaved in and out like an electric eel.

Hughie was a cheeky chap he was.
Waltz round two or three defenders,
And beat the goalie with fluke shot.

Born in Bellshill, he met Alec James,
They played for their school and club teams,
They only separated when they went to different clubs.

P

Hughie was a wanderer, seventeen times transferred,
He cost twenty-seven thousand pounds for his transfers.
This was a record in 1936.

They called him a Papist which he wasn't,
The miscalled names put fight into his blood.
He made many supporters wince.
He had many friends that worshipped him.

They called him a dirty player,
And made him lose his temper.
When he lifted his trousers there was mass of bruises.

Then one day came a train, a spotter knocked him,
"Sorry" was his answer, and he walked on.
Then Hughie saw a train coming and threw himself under it.

The inquest proved it was suicide,
And so ended the life of a gallant footballer,
And he became a legend to the football world.

If you want to try writing one by yourself, or jointly with a group of friends, read some of the ones in Section 7 or in any other books with ballads in them that you can get hold of.

Here are some of the things that make ballads easy to remember and sing, and very dramatic and exciting to listen to.

1. Four line verses with only one rhyme (lines 2 and 4) is the most usual pattern, but ballads don't have to rhyme. You can make them whatever 'shape' you like.
2. They often have bits of conversation in them and the 'he saids' and 'she replieds' are often left out.
3. Lines are often repeated; or there is a chorus which the audience quickly picks up and sings. Sometimes this is a repeated line or verse and sometimes it is nonsense, but is easy to say and carries its meaning in the tune or the way it is said.

Sometimes children set the ballads they make up to tunes that belong to other words. Try this if you are interested.

APPENDIX 8

Childrens' stories today and yesterday

The idea that stories should be written specially for children has grown up in the last two hundred years. Before this, almost all the printed books for children had been 'improving' books because many people from the Puritans onwards had frowned on fairy tales, adventures and romances. They thought these were a waste of time and distracted people, and particularly children, from taking life seriously. So children had to get their stories by listening to parents and servants and old people who told them tales of their own lives and re-told the stories that had been told to them when they were young. But a few of the printed books written for adults became children's favourites. *Pilgrim's Progress* written in 1678 by John Bunyan was one of these. Another favourite was *The Life and Strange Surprising Adventures of Robinson Crusoe* written by Daniel Defoe in 1719, and another was *Gulliver's Travels* written by Jonathan Swift in 1726. The first book of fairy stories to be published came from France about this time and was intended for grown-ups and was very widely read by them. It was called *Tales of Mother Goose; or Stories of Olden Times.* But of course, children got hold of it and the stories are the ones you met when you were younger—Cinderella, Red Riding Hood, Puss-in-Boots and many of the others. In these times, where stories were concerned, adults and children enjoyed the same kinds—fairy tales, fables, adventures and romances.

When people did begin to write stories *specially for children* many of them were 'improving' or 'informative' stories, which seem very strange to us today. There are two of such stories printed in Section 8 pp. 133–137.

Towards the end of Queen Victoria's reign, in the 1870's and 1880's, people began to write straight stories for children without thinking they ought to be improving or informative. *Tom Sawyer* was published in America in 1876; Robert Louis Stevenson wrote *Treasure Island* in 1883 and Edith Nesbit wrote *The Wouldbegoods* in 1901. About the same time the first children's newspapers and comics began to be published, and ever since then there has been a continuous stream of story books written solely for children to enjoy.

Many of these stories are in the shops as paperbacks. New stories written for children and well known children's stories of the past such as *Tom Sawyer* or *Treasure Island* are published in a series called *PUFFIN* books. All of these have a small picture of a Puffin on the spine of the book. Story books produced by this firm for middle-age children are called *PEACOCKS* and for adults, *PENGUINS*.

Choose any book that you have enjoyed and write about it.

If you know why you like it, say so in your account of the book.

Discuss or make a list of the things which make the stories written for children in the early 1800's (printed in Section 8) different from the books you read of your own choosing.

Have you read any of the stories referred to in this Appendix?

What do you think of them? Which of them do you prefer?

Would you have guessed that Pilgrim's Progress, Robinson Cusoe, Gulliver's Travels, Aesop's Fables, and Perrault's and Grimm's Fairy Tales were not written specially for children? Can you find reasons for your opinion?

Some people say that in a scientific age, older children and grown-ups read science-fiction instead of fairy tales. Do you think science-fiction is more like science or more like fiction? Is it at all like fairy tales?

Do you like books that are about people and events today? Or do you think it doesn't much matter where or when the people in the story lived?

Do you prefer to read a story to yourself or to listen to someone else reading or telling a story?

How do stories begin? Look at the beginning of the stories in Section 8. Which one seems to you to have the most promising start?

Look at any story you have written recently and see how good you think the beginning is. Try one or two different beginnings and then decide whether they are better or worse than the original.

APPENDIX 9

How to set out a play-script

Mime and dance drama

Some non-school subjects

You may want to write a play or turn a story into a play, instead of improvising it on the spot.

A Here is part of the opening of a book called *Dr Dolittle's Zoo*.

'Polynesia,' I said, leaning back in my chair and chewing the end of a quill pen, 'What should you say would be the best way to begin another book of Doctor Dolittle's memoirs?'

The old parrot, who was using the glass inkpot on my desk as a mirror, stopped admiring her reflection and glanced at me sharply.

'Another!' she exclaimed. 'Is there going to be *another* Dolittle book?'

'Why—er—yes,' I said. 'After all, we are writing the Doctor's life and we haven't nearly finished yet.'

'Oh, yes, I quite see that,' said Polynesia. 'I was only wondering who decides how many books there are to be.'

'Well, I suppose—in the end—the public does,' said I. 'But tell me now: how would you begin?'

Polynesia pondered a moment.

'What are you calling the book?' she asked presently, screwing up her eyes.

'Doctor Dolittle's Zoo', I said.

'Humph!' she murmured. 'Then I suppose you ought to get on to the zoo part as soon as possible. But first I think you had better put in a little about your own homecoming and your parents and all that.'

B Here it is set out as a play-script.

A play-script consists of dialogue (talk) and stage directions.

Notice (*a*) That the narrative (the story bits) and the description have been left out.

(*b*) Brief hints about what to do are given in the directions to the actors.

(*c*) These stage directions are printed in different type from the dialogue.

(*d*) You don't need to use inverted commas for the talk as you would in a story.

Characters

Hugh Lofting: Author
Polynesia: His parrot

Hugh: Polynesia, what should you say would be the best way to begin another book of Doctor Dolittle's memoirs?

(*Chews end of pen*)

Polynesia: Another! Is there going to be another Dolittle book?

Hugh: Why—er—yes. After all, we are writing the Doctor's life, and we haven't nearly finished yet.

Polynesia: Oh, yes, I quite see that. I was only wondering who decides how many books there shall be.

Hugh: Well, I suppose—in the end—the public does. But tell me, how would you begin?

Polynesia: (*Screwing up her eyes*) What are you calling the book?

Hugh: Doctor Dolittle's Zoo.

Polynesia: Humph! (*Murmurs*) Then I suppose you ought to get on to the zoo part as soon as possible. But first I think you ought to put in a little bit about your own homecoming and your parents and all that. . . .

Mime or dance drama

Sometimes acting without words, or acting with a background of appropriate music can express unusual or mysterious things better than a play with words.

Try making the myth in section 9 into a mime or a dance drama.

Some suggestions:

(a) Read the story again.

(b) Discuss how the characters felt at different points in the story.

(c) Try expressing the feelings of Moksois or Red Leaf in the way you move.

(d) Move slowly so that you have time to express your feelings.

(e) Listen to any records of orchestral music you can find, and choose parts of the record to play which seem to express the same feelings that you want to get into your movements. You might try Sibelius' tone poems, Holst, Wagner, Rachmaninoff, overtures from operas.

Some non-school subjects

When does history start?

If you talk about things that happened yesterday or last week it is usually chat or gossip. It is not until you start enquiring what happened much longer ago that you think of past events as history. Then we want to know what really happened. The further back in time, the less we know, so everything that might tell us about the world a long time ago needs to be looked at.

Thus, as you explore further back in time and further out into the world, and even into space, history, geography and science expand into:

ARCHAEOLOGY: The scientific study of ancient things especially of old buildings, monuments and other remains.

GEOLOGY: The science of the earth's crust.

ANTHROPOLOGY: The science of man, especially of the origin, development, early beliefs, customs, etc., of mankind.

ASTRONOMY: The science of the sun, moon, stars and planets.

Note: The ending -ology means 'the study of'.

See what other words ending in -ology you can collect and find out what they are studies of.

Here are some to start you off:

PALAEONTOLOGY THEOLOGY BIOLOGY PSYCHOLOGY PHYSIOLOGY

APPENDIX 10

All sorts of English

No one speaks in *exactly* the same way as anyone else. Collect any words or expressions which are common in your family but are strange to other people in your class.

People living in different parts of England use different varieties of English. In the West of England for instance, you may hear an obvious cow called 'he'; an old rhyme says:

In Devon all things they be 'he'
Except a Tom-cat and he be 'she'.

Again Scottish English is very different from Norfolk English, or Yorkshire English.

Do any members of your class come from different parts of the British Isles.

Find some of the ways in which their English is different from yours.

These different kinds of English happen naturally, but there are other kinds that people invent in order to have a private language for themselves and their friends which other people won't understand. Here are some examples:

Back slang: You say each word backwards.

e.g. Teem em ni eth dnuorgyalp ta 0.4.
(Meet me in the playground at 4.0.)

or Evah uoy tog eth yadthrib tneserp?
(Have you got the birthday present?)

Pig-Latin: The first consonant is put at the end of the word and -ay added.

e.g. Eetmay emay inay ethay aplay oundgray atay orfay lockay.

Eggy-peggy: -agg is put before each vowel in the middle of words.

e.g. Aggi haggave saggome thagging saggecragget taggo saggay.
(I have something secret to say)

Arague: 'Arag' and any convenient vowel goes in the middle of the word.

e.g. Taragoo baraged, saragays slarageepy haragead,
Taragarry ara wharagile, saragays slaragow,
Paragut aragon therage paragot, saragays grarageedy garagut,
Waragell saragup baragefaragore warage garago.

This means: To bed, says sleepy head,
Tarry a while, says Slow,
Put on the pot, says greedy gut,
We'll sup before we go.

Rhyming slang, sometimes called thieves' language:

Some examples: *I'm going for a ball of chalk with the trouble and strife.*
(I'm going for a walk with the wife)
Tea-leaf: thief.
Almond rocks: socks.
Apples and pears: stairs.
Turtle doves: gloves.

The people above all who needed and used a secret language were thieves and tricksters. Here is a selection from the thieves' language of the 18th century when Bamfylde Carew was King of the Beggars.

Abram: without clothes, naked.
Dimber Damber: chief rogue of a gang.
Doxy: a female rogue.
Autumn: a church.
Autumn divers: church pickpockets.
Autumn bawler: a preacher.
Balsom: money.
Barking irons: pistols.
Beak: magistrate.
Bing: to go e.g. Bing off.
Boarding school: prison.
Cant: thieves' language, sometimes called Pedlars' French.

Cherubims: peevish children who continually cry.
Conefa: a shirt.
Crab shells: shoes.
Darby: ready money, cash.
Darkmans: night
Dimbermost: pretty wench.
Eternity box: coffin.
Flick: to cut e.g. Flick me some panum and cassan (bread and cheese).
Glim: a dark lantern.
Gutter lane: the throat.
Hand-me-downs: second hand clothes.
Hearing cheats: ears.
King's pictures: money.
Libben: private house.
Lightmans: day.
Maunders: beggars.
Misthtopper: coat.
Mutton: women.
Ogles: eyes.
Pad-the-hoof: travel on foot.
Panum: bread.
To peach: to inform.
Reg rag: tongue.
Ruffmans: woods or bushes.
School butter: a beating.
Sharper: a swindler.
Skin-flint: a mean, close man.
Smeller: a nose.
Swiper: an arm.
Stampers: shoes.
Tanner: sixpence.
Tile: a hat.
Tip: to give.
Toggery: clothes.
Vampers: stockings.
Whack: a share.
Whisker: a great lie.
White wool: silver money.
Whip off: to run away.
Womblety Cropt: a hangover.

Some of these words from the canting (or secret) thieves' language have now got themselves into the language that anyone uses. Can you find any of these?

If you are interested, try writing a conversation between two beggars making their way towards their known lodging house for the night. Use as many of their special words as you can.

As well as all these private kinds of English that are used in Great Britain, there are many other kinds of English used by people who have come from outside the British Isles such as North America, The West Indies, Europe, India, even China or a South Sea Island. Wherever they come from, the English they speak will be different from yours, just as yours is different from that of people who come from another part of England.

In the South Sea Islands a kind of English called Pidgin English is spoken.

Here are some examples:

Man he write he stop long machine belong write.
(The man is always writing.)

Capsize him coffee long cup!
(Pour coffee into the cup.)

All the time all the time Mary belong me he throw out.
(My wife is always being sick.)

And here is the story of the angel telling the Shepherds to go to Bethlehem to see Mary and the baby Jesus.

All watchman belong sheep-sheep he adore him Jesus

Long this-fellow night Mary he carry him pikinini Jesus, he got some-fellow man he watch long sheep-sheep close to long Bethlehem. Now all he look him one-fellow angel he come down long all. All he lookim him, all he fraid. Angel he speak:

'You-fellow no fraid! Me bringim good-fellow talk long you-fellow. Now long night long place belong David Christ, he master, him he come down finish long all man. You-fellow go, by 'n' by you findim pikinini he sleep long crib.'

Angel he talk finish, now plenty angel he come down he stop one time long this-fellow angel, all he honourim God, all he sing-sing:

'Honour long God on top, good-fellow time long all 'gether good-fellow man long ground!'

All angel he go finish, now all watchmen he speak:

'Go on, you-me go long Bethlehem, you-me look savvy long this-fellow talk long God.'

All he go, all he findim Maria two-fellow Joseph one time pikinini him he sleep he stop long box. All he lookim Jesus finish, all he go back, all he honourim God, thankim him, long something all he lookim long this-fellow night.

Discuss how Pidgin works as a language. It has perfectly sensible rules but because it is so simplified it has to go to a long way round to say what it wants to.

Here are two examples of school boys' attempts to describe first a piano, and second a petrol pump.

Big-fellow box you fight him he cry out.
Big-fellow worm he squirt funny water, you lightim match you see angel.

Now try out some Pidgin for yourselves.

One of the best ways of learning to use your own kind of English well is to try to use other people's English.

ACKNOWLEDGEMENTS

The author gratefully acknowledges permission to reproduce extracts from the following copyright material.

Claude Blanguernon: 'The Lion, the Hyena and the Jackal' from *Le Hoggar*. Reprinted by permission of Editions Arthaud

Henri Bosco: *The Boy and the River* trans. Gerard Hopkins. Reprinted by permission of Oxford University Press

Bouba and Jacques: 'This is My Home' and 'The Day we were Herdsmen' from *The Birth of a Dialogue between Africa and Europe* (U.N.E.S.C.O.)

ACKNOWLEDGEMENTS

Walter de la Mare: 'Rain' from *The Complete Poems of Walter de la Mare*. Reprinted by permission of The Literary Trustees of Walter de la Mare and the Society of Authors as their representative

Leonard de Vries: 'Peter Piper's Polite Preface' and woodcuttings from *Flowers of Delight*. Reprinted by permission of Dennis Dobson

Gerald Durrell: 'Lessons with George' from *My Family and Other Animals*. Reprinted by permission of Rupert Hart-Davis Ltd.

Maxim Gorki: *My Childhood* trans. I. Schneider. Reprinted by permission of Paul Elek Productions Ltd.

Robert Graves: 'Dicky' from *The Penny Fiddle*. Reprinted by permission of Mr. Graves and Cassell and Co. Ltd.

Ted Hughes: 'The Thought Fox' from *The Hawk in the Rain*. Reprinted by permission of Faber and Faber Ltd. and Harper and Row, Publishers, copyright © 1957 by Ted Hughes. 'Capturing Animals' from *Poetry in the Making*. Reprinted by permission of Faber and Faber Ltd. *The Price of a Bride*. Reprinted by permission of Miss O. Hughes

Herbert Kohl: 'What a Block' from *Teaching the Unteachable*. Reprinted from *The New York Review of Books*. Copyright © 1966 by Herbert Kohl

D. H. Lawrence: 'When I went to the Circus' from *The Complete Poems of D. H. Lawrence* (William Heinemann Ltd.) Reprinted by permission of Laurence Pollinger Ltd. and the Estate of the late Mrs. Frieda Lawrence

Laurie Lee: *Cider with Rosie* (The Hogarth Press Ltd.) Reprinted by permission of Laurence Pollinger Ltd.

Frank B. Linderman: Extracts from *Plenty-Coups, Chief of the Crows*. Reprinted by permission of the University of Nebraska Press

Vachel Lindsay: 'The Flower-Fed Buffaloes' from *Going to the Stars*. Reprinted by permission of Appleton-Century affiliate of Meredith Press. Copyright 1926, D. Appleton & Co. Copyright renewed 1954 by Elizabeth C. Lindsay

Hugh Lofting: *Dr. DoLittle's Zoo* (Jonathan Cape Ltd.) Reprinted by permission of the Executors of the Hugh Lofting Estate and Mr. C. Lofting

John A. and Alan Lomax: 'Buffalo Skinners' Folksong and Music from *Folk Song U.S.A.* Copyright 1947 by John A. and Alan Lomax. Reprinted by permission of Duell, Sloan and Pearce, affiliate of Meredith Press

Konrad Z. Lorenz: 'Cat' from *Man Meets Dog* and 'Jackdaw' from *King Solomon's Ring*. Reprinted by permission of Associated Book Publishers Ltd.

Amy Lowell: 'Night Clouds' from *The Complete Poetical Works of Amy Lowell*. Reprinted by permission of Houghton Mifflin Co.

John Manifold: 'The Griesly Wife' from *Selected Verse*. Copyright © 1946 by John Day Co. Inc., Publisher

Bill Naughton: 'Flying the Kite' from *One Small Boy*. Reprinted by permission of MacGibbon and Kee Ltd.

Frank O'Connor: 'The Idealist' from *Stories of Frank O'Connor*. Reprinted by permission of A. D. Peters & Co.

Ed. Grace Jackson Penney: 'How the Seven Brothers saved their Sister' from *Tales of the Cheyenne*. Reprinted by permission of Houghton Mifflin Co. and Mrs. Grace Jackson Penney

Marcel Proust: *Swann's Way* trans. C. K. Scott-Moncrieff. Reprinted by permission of Mr. George Scott-Moncrieff and Chatto and Windus Ltd.

James Reeves: 'Boating' from *The Blackbird in the Lilac*. Reprinted by permission of Oxford University Press

Theodore Roethke: 'Night Crow' from *Collected Poems*. 'Night Crow' copyright 1944 by Saturday Review Association Inc. Reprinted by permission of Doubleday & Co. Inc. and Faber and Faber Ltd.

W. W. E. Ross: 'The Diver' from *Penguin Book of Canadian Verse*. Reprinted by permission of Penguin Books Ltd.

William Saroyan: 'The Summer of the Beautiful White Horse' from *My Name is Aram* (Faber and Faber Ltd.) Copyright 1938, 1966 by William Saroyan. Reprinted by permission of Harcourt, Brace and World Inc. and Laurence Pollinger Ltd. 'The Great Leapfrog Contest' from *The Insurance Salesman and Other Stories* (Faber and Faber Ltd.) Reprinted by permission of Laurence Pollinger Ltd. and Mr. W. Saroyan

Dylan Thomas: Extract from *Portrait of the Artist as a Young Dog*. Reprinted by permission of J. M. Dent & Son Ltd. and the Trustees for the Copyrights of the late Dylan Thomas

James Thurber: 'The White Rabbit Caper' from *Vintage Thurber*. Copyright © 1963. Hamish Hamilton, London. Reprinted by permission of the publisher. Copyright © 1953 James Thurber. From *Thurber Country* published by Simon and Schuster, New York. Originally printed in *The New Yorker*

Leo Tolstoy: 'We Play Games' from *Childhood, Boyhood, Youth*. Reprinted by permission of Penguin Books Ltd.

Monique Wittig: 'The Ghost in the Forest' from *The Opoponax*. English translation © 1966 by Simon and Schuster Inc. Reprinted by permission of Simon & Schuster Inc. and Peter Owen Ltd.

The author would also like to thank the following for permission to reprint their poems and prose pieces:

The Daily Mirror Children's Literary Competition for 'Dog with a Million Fleas' by Stuart, 'The True Story of a Little Sparrow' by Angela and 'A Memory' by Dianne. Alan, Anna, Anna, Celia, Celia, David, Ian, John, John, Peter, R. Quarrington, Richard, Ron, Rosalind, Ross and Richard, Sarah, Susie.

The author would also like to thank the many friends who have contributed writing done by their pupils and who have tried out some of the suggestions in this book. Thanks are due also to members of the London Association for the Teaching of English and to colleagues in the English Department at the London Institute of Education. The ideas about English teaching which are embodied in the book are to a large extent the product of discussions and work together over a long period.

The Publishers thank the following for permission to reproduce photographs: Ashmolean Museum, Oxford: page 128; Euan Duff: 80, 140; *Flowers of Delight* by Leonard de Vries, Courtesy of Publisher: 135, 137, 166, 168, 171; Jane Gate: 30, 36, 70, 87, 112, 117, 139, 144, 202, and the cover; Henry Grant: 25, 34; John Hilleson: 44, 187, 190; Mansell Collection: 132; 151, 175, 177; Roger Mayne: 54, 75, 98, 194; Museum of Primitive Art, New York: 158; L. Hugh Newman: 106; Graham Salmon: 43; John Massey Stewart: 8, 19, 96.

INDEX